The Aerofilms Book of
LONDON FROM THE AIR

The Aerofilms Book of
LONDON FROM THE AIR

Paul Johnson

HOLT, RINEHART AND WINSTON
NEW YORK

Photographs copyright © 1984 Aerofilms Ltd
Text copyright © 1984 Paul Johnson

Published in the United States by
Holt, Rinehart and Winston, 383 Madison Avenue,
New York, New York 10017.

Originally published in Great Britain.

Library of Congress Cataloging in Publication Data
Johnson, Paul, 1928–
    The aerofilms book of London from the air.
    1. London (England)—Description—1981– —Views.
2. London (England)—Aerial photographs.   I. Title.
II. Title: London from the air.
DA684.25.J64 1984 914.21′0022′2 84–6705

ISBN: 0–03–071918–6

First American Edition
Printed in Italy
10 9 8 7 6 5 4 3 2 1

Designed by Simon Bell and Joy FitzSimmons
Typeset by Keyspools Ltd, Golborne, Lancashire, England
Colour separations by Newsele Litho Ltd
Printed and bound by LEGO, Vicenza, Italy

ISBN 0-03-071918-6

INTRODUCTION

Surveying a great city like London from the air, one concentrates inevitably on its purely visual characteristics, reflecting its physical structure. But such a structure, in turn, reflects the dynamics and statics of history: that is, the interplay of great historical forces with the huge continuities of economic geography and institutional tradition. The first thing we notice about the physical structure of London, which is now about 1,930 years old, is that the area of densest development is still the area of original settlement. The core of London has not changed its location in nearly two millennia.

The Romans founded London about AD 50, shortly after they began their conquest of the island. The site was deliberately chosen as a defensible commercial centre, above the high-tide mark but suitable for a bridge, with a natural plateau on the north bank of the bridge which could be settled and walled. Roman judgement was vindicated not only by the fact that the town of 330 acres (large by the standards of antiquity) flourished for nearly four hundred years under their rule, but also by the extraordinary stability of its commercial centre. The two main west–east streets of the Roman town still underly the street-plan of the City; the old Roman market-place is the heart of the present-day financial district; and immediately north of the main Roman temple is the great crossroads in front of the Bank of England and the Mansion House, the hub from which radiate the eight spokes which form the City's inner wheel. All this is revealed plainly by aerial photography.

There must, in fact, have been continuity of settlement, and to some extent of function, even in the darkest years of the Saxon invasions. The Romans had built huge walls which survived, even if in bad repair. The Anglo-Saxon Chronicle, for the year 456–7, says that after Hengist fought the Britons and killed 4,000 of them, 'the Britons then deserted Kent and fled with great fear to London'. So the effect of the invasions was, if anything, to reinforce London's position, and though of course the Saxons eventually absorbed the London area, the town continued as a major commercial centre except for a brief period after the Danes took and sacked it in the ninth century. Then, with King Alfred's victory, the markets were restored and the walls rebuilt, and by this time London again had a serviceable bridge, virtually on the site of its Roman predecessor.

The first of the seven great historic convulsions which have created London as we know it occurred in the eleventh century. In earlier Saxon times London was politically no more than the chief town of a tribal confederacy, though plainly its commercial importance grew steadily. There was, however, an important royal monastic foundation on the banks of the Thames, west of London at Thorney Island, the island of thorns, and in the mid-eleventh century Edward the Confessor determined to re-endow it on such a scale as to make it the principal religious foundation in the country. To mark its intimate connection with the royal line of Wessex, he not only began to build an enormous Romanesque abbey there, on the lines of the latest Cluniac churches, but effectively transferred his capital from Winchester to the new Westminster by building a palace alongside the abbey. The latter was completed just before his death, early in 1066, and the new Norman king, William the Conqueror, anxious to emphasize his claim to be Edward's true heir, and his fidelity to the Confessor's intentions, had himself crowned in the new abbey and built a formidable stone fort of a revolutionary design at the south-east corner of the London wall. His son, Rufus, confirmed the position of Westminster–London as the political, administrative and commercial capital of the country by building a vast hall at Westminster – probably the biggest royal hall in Europe – and, almost certainly, by establishing his central exchequer alongside it. Westminster Hall became the principal location of the royal courts of justice. Hence by the end of the eleventh century the paramountcy of London in the urban life of the nation had been decisively established.

Until the seventeenth century London was effectively a walled city with defensible gates and other strongpoints. William the Conqueror's White Tower grew into one of the strongest concentric castles in Europe, never taken by storm. All this inhibited urban sprawl, and throughout the Middle Ages, and indeed right up to the end of the sixteenth century, the City changed its configuration very little. It acquired a growing measure of self-government from the 1130s onward, its population rose to about 20,000 at the end of the fourteenth century, and its wealth continued to increase; but it remained a city of wood, with an almost unaltered street-plan. However, the presence of Westminster, the political and administrative capital of the kingdom, only four miles up the river, inevitably meant that the intervening ground was settled and developed. Until the late eighteenth century the main means of transport within the London area was the river-boat, and so the great lords, ecclesiastical and secular, built their town palaces near the river, with gardens running down to riverside landing-stages. A few were on the south bank – the Bishop of Winchester at Southwark, the Archbishop of Canterbury at Lambeth. But most were on the strip of north bank between the City and Westminster: Arundel House, John of Gaunt's great palace at the Savoy, the palaces of the Dukes of Somerset and Northumberland, and of the Bishop of Durham and the Archbishop of York. Thus the two centres were slowly connected, and a host of humble folk built tenements around the great men's houses, and indeed in and around Westminster Palace itself – the slums of Westminster still existed in the first half of the nineteenth century and were graphically described by Dickens in *Our Mutual Friend*. A little inland, Fleet Street emerged from the City's Temple Bar to become the Strand, that is the street nearest the river-bank, the main artery to Westminster, which quickly generated a system of side-streets on either side.

Such developments were gradual. In the 1530s, however, there occurred the second of London's great convulsions when Henry VIII dissolved the religious houses and acquired their real estate for the Crown. Collectively the Church owned a fifth of the land of England; and religious foundations and bishoprics owned perhaps half the land which surrounded the City of London itself. These possessions constituted a sort of green belt, since ecclesiastics were very conservative landlords who preferred to maintain large market gardens, even near the centres of cities, rather than develop them into domestic housing. When Henry VIII broke up the monastic system he released an enormous amount of prime urban land on to the commercial market, which in due course accelerated the expansion of London outside the City walls and into the suburbs.

It is true he created a green belt of his own, out of the arable, horticultural and indeed marshland he acquired in west London as a result of the seizures. He knocked together something like a thousand acres, much of it from the estates of the Abbots of Westminster, and from them constructed the new Palace of St James and a series of enclosed deer parks. They now make up the great complex of open spaces we know as St James's Park, Green Park, Buckingham Palace Gardens and Hyde Park-Kensington Gardens. The Earl of Chatham called them 'the lungs of London' and they remain the capital's most precious amenities. Henry VIII also took the properties of Cardinal Wolsey on the north bank near Westminster, and turned them into the vast, sprawling Palace of Whitehall, so that by the end of his reign the whole topography of western London had been transformed.

Henry VIII was a great spender, always in need of quick cash, so much of the Church land he acquired was soon disposed of or leased, and the carve-up became the ultimate basis of most of the great London aristocratic estates. Lay landlords were less likely to preserve open spaces than their ecclesiastical predecessors. For instance, Hatton Garden, called after the Elizabethan courtier who got the Queen to squeeze it out of the Bishopric of Ely in the 1570s, was then a huge kitchen-garden (reputed to produce the best strawberries in the world), a seven-acre vineyard and five acres of arable; under lay ownership it developed into an industrial suburb of the City. Again, Covent (or Convent) Garden, which the Abbots of Westminster owned on the north-west edge of the City, was acquired by the Russells, Earls of Bedford, and in the 1630s the fourth Earl, in conjunction with Inigo Jones, developed it as London's first proper square, modelled partly on the piazza at Leghorn (where there was already an English mercantile colony) and partly on Henri IV's Place des Vosges in Paris. Lincoln's Inn Fields was laid out at about the same time, and soon after the Restoration, in 1665, Lord St Albans began building St James's Square, the first of the West End squares.

A year later, on 2 September 1666, followed the third convulsion in London's history. The Great Fire began in Pudding Lane off Thames Street and burned for four days and nights; it darkened the sun as far west as Oxford, and ash fell at Windsor. It seems to have killed only six people but it burned down an oblong of a mile and a half by half a mile, that is 373 acres within the walls and 63 acres outside them. Of the City's 107 churches 84 were entirely destroyed, plus 44 out of 51 City Livery Halls. Sir Christopher Wren designed a new, planned City to replace the old one, with embanked *quais* and terraces along the Thames, a gridiron network of streets and six tremendous piazzas. Little came of it, but at least he was given the chance to build a completely new cathedral to replace the gutted St Paul's. Thanks to his genius, and his extraordinary courage and energy, he not only designed a masterpiece, but lived to see it completed. He also produced 51 new City churches, a variety of new public buildings like Temple Bar, palatial schemes at either end of the metropolis – Greenwich Hospital, the Royal Hospital Chelsea and the vast new quadrangle at Hampton Court – and, not least, gave rise to a new generation of gifted architects, led by Nicholas Hawksmoor, who gave London and its new suburbs a fresh group of brilliant churches.

The convulsion of the fire thus gave birth not indeed to a planned baroque city, but to a superb new skyline, dominated by St Paul's great dome and the spires, cupolas and towers of Wren's churches, a skyline which was to remain London's outstanding visual characteristic for 250 years, until the Second World War. And in between the churches a new London arose, a London of red brick and classical shapes. Old London had been a wooden city, with stone as a luxury material for public projects such as the first stone London Bridge, built in the last quarter of the twelfth century. The best stone was imported from Caen in Normandy. This was what William the Conqueror used for his White Tower, and Henry VIII was still shipping it to London in the 1530s and 1540s for use at Hampton Court and elsewhere. But in the early seventeenth century, under royal patronage, the quarries of the Isle of Portland off the Dorset coast were developed, and Portland stone, 'the King of the Oolites', became London's premium building material. Wren used it in vast quantities for St Paul's, and much trouble it cost him, for the quarrymen of the Isle formed an ancient and surly trade union, and other contractors tried to horn in on Wren's royal monopoly. There was not enough Portland to go round, quite apart from the expense. London lay well to the south-east of the limestone belt which runs diagonally across England from Dorset to Lincolnshire. So developers turned to brick. It had been first used in quantity in the fifteenth century. From the late seventeenth century it became almost universal in London, and gave to the capital its detailed physiognomy.

The new face of London was also the product of the fourth great convulsion in its history; it might be termed the systematic development of aristocratic estates. In the Middle Ages the wealthy had found it convenient, and believed it also salutary, to live by the river. Even by the early sixteenth century, however, those who wanted big gardens and clear waters, like Sir Thomas More, had to push as far west as Chelsea. From the second quarter of the seventeenth century, the rich began moving west, away from the river, into St James's, Holborn and beyond, helped by the new taste for squares and formal developments. In the last years of the seventeenth century, the ancient house of Berkeley developed south-east Mayfair; the north-east followed soon after 1700, laid out by Sir Richard Grosvenor, whose mother Mary Davies had brought as dowry the Manor of Ebury. The Russells followed with the spacious development of Bloomsbury. North of Oxford Street, development was in the hands of the Harleys, Earls of Oxford, and the Cavendish-Bentincks, Dukes of Portland; to these, in the second half of the eighteenth century, were added the Portman estates, developed from the ancient Manor of Lilestone in St Marylebone. In the 1770s, the Cadogans began to develop the Sloane Street area, and from the 1820s onwards the Grosvenors laid out their estate south of Hyde Park to form Belgravia. In the meantime, the Crown estates had created Regent's Park and the magnificent terraces surrounding it.

In the expansion of London from the Restoration until about the 1850s, the main work was done by these great estates. There were about 35 of them, mostly of the nobility, though with a few church or educational foundations too. They were not quite as conservative as the old religious houses, but they did think in the long-term: they employed first-class architects as a rule, aimed at low density, and usually exercised strict and benevolent control over what their leaseholders did. Their major squares were often gated and guarded. If all these planned squares – St James's, Covent Garden, Grosvenor, Berkeley, Hanover, Montagu, Cavendish, Bedford, Belgrave, Cadogan, Eaton, Chester, and perhaps a dozen more, had been preserved as they were originally planned and built, London must now surely be the most beautiful city in the world. But a lay-owned estate is inevitably more vulnerable than an ecclesiastical one. Failure of heirs, extravagance and sales, and from the 1890s onwards the merciless erosion of death-duties, gradually loosened the grip of the big London families. In consequence, piecemeal rebuilding and development took place. Of all the great squares, only Bedford Square remains in its original state; many have been totally rebuilt. The grandiose schemes of the Crown have also been ruined: the *via triumphalis* Nash built under the Prince Regent, from Carlton House Terrace to Regent's Park, was quite destroyed by the episodic development of Portland Place and Regent Street. The whittling down of the aristocratic London estates was followed, in the first half of the twentieth century, by the demolition and rebuilding (usually for hotels, flats, shops and offices) of the town palaces of the nobility. The last to fall was Londonderry House, Park Lane, in the 1960s; now only Spencer House, St James's, remains intact in family hands.

These changes, however, were gradual; far more dramatic – the fifth great convulsion to shake London – was the coming of the railways from the 1830s onwards. The aim of the great trunk railways was to push their railheads, and build their terminals and marshalling yards, as close to the commercial heart of London as possible. They proceeded by private Acts of Parliament, which gave them wide powers of compulsory purchase. But the big, rich London estates could and did fight back, so that the companies tended to drive their line of rail through the poorer parts of London, and build their terminals in working-class districts. Where they could not penetrate at all they began, from the 1860s on, to build an underground network. Hence aerial photographs of London, where the rail network stands out more clearly than the roads – almost as clearly as the waterways, in fact – show a curious contrast. The whole of west-central London, the entire West End and middle-class Kensington, have no railway lines at all (except underground ones). The lines from the north and west ended at Euston and Paddington, in the south at Victoria. In north, east and south London, however, the rail networks are the most prominent features of all, save the river itself. Despite some post-1945 closures, they occupy enormous areas and blight whole districts, especially in the south and east. In *Dombey and Son*, Dickens described in some harrowing passages the destruction of entire working-class neighbourhoods involved in the construction of the Euston railhead. Aerial photographs alone convey the magnitude of the change brought about by the growth of 'Railway London' in the Euston-St Pancras-King's Cross district; a change which can be paralleled in the Bishopsgate-Broad Street-Liverpool Street-Fenchurch Street area of east London, and on the south bank east of London Bridge and south of Victoria. Some of these juggernaut railways, which wiped out historic districts and dispossessed perhaps half a million Londoners (usually without compensation) embodied duplicate routes, and in the end proved needless. From start to finish, the construction of London's railway network proceeded without central planning.

Yet does planning work any better than laissez-faire? The question needs to be asked in the light of London's experience since 1945. The German blitz, 1940–5, was the sixth of the great convulsions to shake London. The bombing caused immense damage in every part of the capital, but it was most comprehensive in the City (where it destroyed a third of all buildings), in the traditional East End, and in the dock areas of Stepney, Poplar and Rotherhithe. As after the Great Fire of 1666, an immense opportunity for a comprehensive and enlightened plan of rebuilding presented itself. Alas, there was no plan; no Wren either. What was produced was the Town and Country Planning Act of 1947. In theory this subjected London to the strictest planning regulations, conceived from the most high-minded motives, of any city in Europe. In practice, what it produced was a great speculative property boom, beginning in the 1950s and continuing until the recession of the late 1970s. It left central, north, south-west and east London littered with concrete and glass office blocks of almost unrelieved mediocrity. Meanwhile, London local government replaced the blitzed or obsolete terraces with vast, alien housing estates, often dominated by menacing tower-blocks. Aerial photographs pitilessly map the lost opportunity to rebuild London as a fair and rational city. Indeed, in all the rebuilding, London failed to acquire even a planned road network, just as in the nineteenth century it had failed to provide itself with planned railways. The failure of the London authorities has, indeed, been most comprehensive when they have attempted, as at the Elephant and Castle, to integrate major new building schemes with road-planning. Hence, the post-1945 rebuilding phase may fairly be described as the seventh and last of the great convulsions to grip London;

and perhaps the most unfortunate and destructive of them all.

Yet in some important respects London has improved steadily in recent decades, and this too is revealed in the photographs. Post-war legislation to clean London's air and waterways has been unexpectedly successful. The Thames is now a cleaner river than it was in Shakespeare's day; it has lost its odious brown colour and its summer-time stench; indeed in recent years salmon have been caught in Thames Valley tributaries, which means they must have braved the lower reaches. Even more important is the effect of smokeless fuel and other restrictions on London's air, which has meant the end of what Dickens in *Bleak House* termed 'the London particular', the dense, yellow-grey coal-smoke fog which was last seen in the early 1950s.

The reduction in smoke-pollution has also made practical the cleaning of London's buildings. From the 1960s onwards we have begun to see, for the first time, the pristine beauty of our great stone monuments. The majesty of St Paul's has been enhanced; the wonderful detail of Westminster Abbey stonework has been revealed. Many Victorian buildings hitherto dismissed, behind their soot, as mediocre – in Whitehall for example – are now seen as well worth scrutiny; and cleaning has exposed the merits not merely of stonework but the colour effects of polished brick, brick and stone, terracotta and tile, as in the Prudential Building, Westminster Cathedral, the Law Courts and the Natural History Museum. At the top end of the scale, the Houses of Parliament have emerged from the grime as an undoubted and intricate masterpiece. Hence, if the London which presents herself in these photographs is a battered beauty who has lost many of her ancient charms, she is at least recovering her natural coloration, and it is on the whole a fair one. The pictures which follow constitute a balance-sheet of London's profit and loss over recent decades; and they give a unique insight into its structures, produced by two thousand years of crowded history.

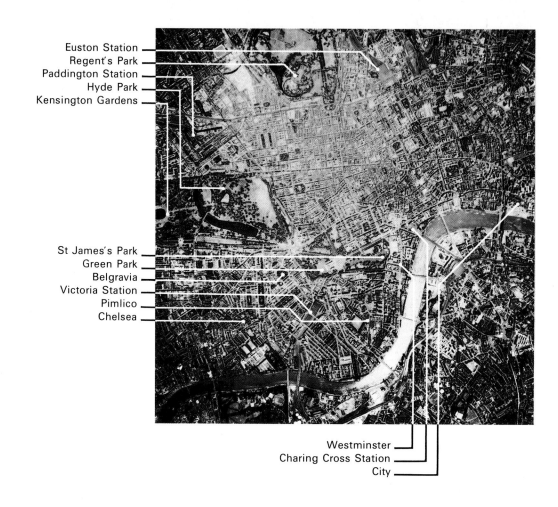

Euston Station
Regent's Park
Paddington Station
Hyde Park
Kensington Gardens

St James's Park
Green Park
Belgravia
Victoria Station
Pimlico
Chelsea

Westminster
Charing Cross Station
City

CENTRAL LONDON

This high-altitude photograph brings out key characteristics in London's history. First, it is remarkable that Roman London, north of the river on the far right, is still the area of most intensive development, illustrating the extraordinary stability of the original City core. Second, the big loop forming Westminster emerges clearly. This grew up in the tenth and eleventh centuries as a quite separate royal and ecclesiastical centre to London. But, as it was so close to the City, it was inevitable that the open country between them should be developed. Hence London's westward expansion during the Middle Ages and Tudor times. Henry VIII prevented this drift to the west producing a formless urban agglomerate by corralling together about 1,000 acres of mainly Church land and enclosing them as a series of parks. As the picture shows, they still form a decisive green area running across the centre of west London. Once Westminster and London were united, expansion turned to the north, but here again the

efforts of the Prince Regent and his architect John Nash to create a *rus in urbe* north of Marylebone prevented megalopolitan sprawl: the inner and outer circles of Regent's Park can be plainly seen. South of Henry VIII's green belt of parks, early in the nineteenth century, Belgravia and Pimlico grew up to expand into Kensington and link up with Chelsea village. The photo also reveals the extent to which the wealthier parts of west-central and west London, formed largely by the great aristocratic estate-developments, were able to protect themselves from devastation during the mid-nineteenth-century railway age. The rich estates fought off the railway companies so that the railways could not penetrate further south than Euston and Paddington, or further north than Victoria, with Charing Cross their furthest penetration from the east. Throughout London's West End, the rails were banned or forced underground.

St Katharine's Dock
Tower of London
Custom House
Cornhill
Eastcheap
Monument
Lombard Street
Adelaide House
Fishmongers' Hall
London Bridge
Lower Thames Street
Cannon Street Station

Hay's Wharf
HMS Belfast
Tower Bridge
Southwark Cathedral
Tooley Street
London Bridge Station

LONDON BRIDGE

London did not exist before the Romans came in AD 43, and it began literally with London Bridge. They flung it across the Thames probably about AD 50 at a spot just above the (then) tidal limit. The site was carefully chosen: flat sands and semi-marshland on the southern, Southwark side, but on the north 40-foot high hills leading to a plateau, bisected by small streams like the Fleet and the Walbrook. There they built a planned commercial centre of 330 acres which was eventually (c AD 200) surrounded by a nine-foot thick wall. The Governor's palace occupied most of what is now Cannon Street Station. From it a Roman road ran along the future Eastcheap to the eastern extremity of the wall at the Tower of London. A second main street ran alongside Cheapside and on its north side, between Lombard Street and Cornhill, was a huge market place or Forum, and a Basilica, about half as long as St Paul's, which served as a town hall and court. So the commercial centre of the City of London has scarcely shifted at all in nineteen centuries. Nor has London Bridge, give or take thirty yards on either side. The original Roman bridge, of wood,

may have survived into Saxon times; at any rate there was certainly a wooden Saxon bridge there in about 980, when a woman was flung off it for witchcraft. The Norsemen pulled it down in 1014, by roping the piers to their prows and then rowing backwards downstream with the tide. Thus they gave birth to the oldest London nursery rhyme: 'London Bridge is falling down'. Then followed a succession of wooden bridges eventually (1209) replaced by a stone one which took 30 years to build and cost 150 lives. It had 19 arches and a drawbridge and was gradually covered by shops, houses and a chapel. Many famous Londoners, including Hogarth, lived there, until the houses were cleared by Act of Parliament, 1756–63. But the bridge itself remained until New London Bridge, designed by John Rennie, was finished in 1831. Then the old bridge, which had served over 600 years, was pulled down. The New Bridge was itself replaced, 1967–72, by Lord Holford's three-span cantilever, and Rennie's masterpiece was dismantled and re-erected in the holiday resort of Lake Havasu City, Arizona.

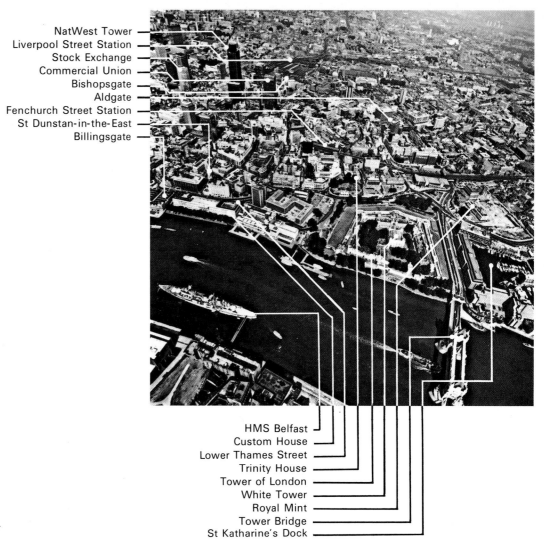

NatWest Tower —
Liverpool Street Station —
Stock Exchange —
Commercial Union —
Bishopsgate —
Aldgate —
Fenchurch Street Station —
St Dunstan-in-the-East —
Billingsgate —

HMS Belfast —
Custom House —
Lower Thames Street —
Trinity House —
Tower of London —
White Tower —
Royal Mint —
Tower Bridge —
St Katharine's Dock —

THE HEART OF THE CITY

Both Anglo-Saxon and Norman London grew up on top of the Roman city, and the old walls were gradually replaced by medieval masonry. The walls had six gates. Just north of Fenchurch Street Station was Aldgate, leading east to Colchester. Near Liverpool Street Station was Bishopsgate, going north to York. Cripplegate and Aldersgate also led north, Newgate west, and Ludgate to Westminster. About half the medieval city can be seen in this picture: it housed 20,000 people, divided into over 100 parishes and served by as many as 120 churches. Fewer than a dozen remain; indeed, apart from the Tower itself, there are few medieval buildings left in the City. The fire of 1666 destroyed much; German Second World War bombers did their bit; but the City itself has always been quick to pull down the obsolete, for it is a very commercial place. This is the heart of commercial London. Just north of the Tower is Trinity House (1792–4) by Samuel Wyatt, whose Elder Brethren look after all British lighthouses. Winston Churchill

was proud to wear their uniform, once telling a startled Frenchman, who asked what it was: '*Je suis un frère ainé de la Sainte Trinité*'. To the left is the long façade of the Custom House (1825) by David Laing and Sir Robert Smirke and beyond it the original home of Billingsgate fish market, where the four-letter word was reputedly invented. This stretch of river below London Bridge, now dominated by the Second World War cruiser HMS *Belfast*, was once the busiest on the entire river. So when it was decided to build a bridge by the Tower, the last on the Thames, Parliament laid down (1885) that it must allow a passage for ships 200 feet and 135 high. It also stipulated that the design must be Gothic. The result was the masterpiece known as Tower Bridge, created by the engineer Sir John Wolfe Barry and the architect Sir Horace Jones. The superb hydraulic machinery used to raise the vast bascules remains but since 1976 it has been worked by electricity.

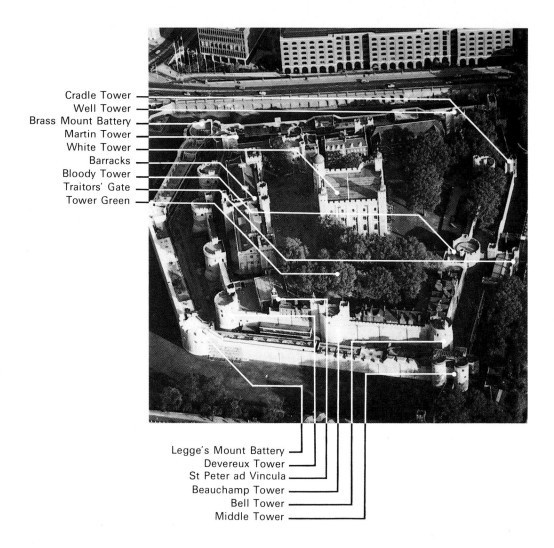

Cradle Tower
Well Tower
Brass Mount Battery
Martin Tower
White Tower
Barracks
Bloody Tower
Traitors' Gate
Tower Green

Legge's Mount Battery
Devereux Tower
St Peter ad Vincula
Beauchamp Tower
Bell Tower
Middle Tower

THE TOWER OF LONDON

The Tower is on the site of an ancient Roman bastion but it covers a much bigger area, 18 acres, and is essentially the work of William the Conqueror and his brilliant master-builder, Gundulf Bishop of Rochester. Gundulf had been in the Holy Land and seen the great square keep the Byzantines had built at Sayun. So in 1079 he began building an even bigger and stronger one in London, with walls 15 feet wide at the base and 11 feet at the top, held together by mortar 'tempered with the blood of beasts'. Blood has been the constant theme of this fortress, though the keep itself, plastered and whitewashed, has always been known as the White Tower. The actual Bloody Tower, just behind Traitor's Gate, is later, one of the thirteen towers in the wall put up by Henry III and Edward I in the thirteenth century to protect the Inner Ward. There was an outer wall in addition, two moats and a huge barbican; the castle was so strong it never fell by storm. But it was more than a fortress: for centuries it was a treasury, a depot for state records, a royal zoo and an armoury. It was a palace too.

By tradition, each monarch spent the night there before the coronation, then processed through the City to Westminster Abbey to be crowned. But Elizabeth I was the last to observe this custom. James I declined, and when told he ought to 'show himself to the people', threatened to 'take down my breeks and show them my arse'. Above all the Tower was a prison and the scene of innumerable executions, both legal and unofficial. Two kings were murdered there: Henry VI and the young Edward V, together with his brother (in the Bloody Tower). In the beautiful sixteenth-century church of St Peter ad Vincula lie the remains of the Dukes of Somerset and Northumberland and two of Henry VIII's wives, Anne Boleyn and Catherine Howard, all four beheaded. Even Elizabeth I had a spell in prison, using the room in the Bell Tower once occupied by St Thomas More, executed by her father. Twentieth-century prisoners have included Sir Roger Casement (1916) and Rudolf Hess (1941).

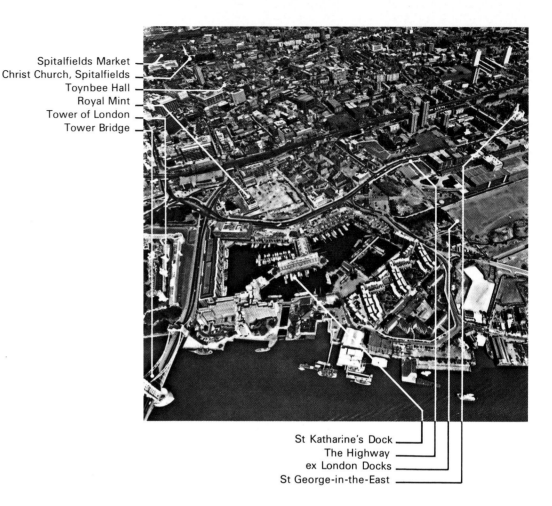

Spitalfields Market

Christ Church, Spitalfields

Toynbee Hall

Royal Mint

Tower of London

Tower Bridge

St Katharine's Dock

The Highway

ex London Docks

St George-in-the-East

ST KATHARINE'S DOCK

The East End starts with the territory beyond the Tower of London, though the Royal Mint, just north-east of it, forms an outer salient of the City. There were suburbs of the poor here even in the Middle Ages, though the real expansion began in Elizabethan times. At the end of the sixteenth century Stow said he could still remember when it was green fields, though now 'a continuous building throughout'. Thereafter the steady expansion of trade, and of the docks to accommodate the thousands of ships which came to London annually, led to the creation of a huge slum population. By the end of the nineteenth century over 300,000 people lived in the ancient country parish of Stepney. From the early eighteenth century efforts were made to cope with this social problem. Nicholas Hawksmoor was commissioned to build a series of East End churches and produced three masterpieces. Two of them can be seen in this picture: Christ Church (1723–9) near Spitalfields Market, and St George-in-the-East

(1715–23) off the Cannon Street Road. In the nineteenth century came high-minded 'slumming', centred on Toynbee Hall in Commercial Street, founded in 1884 for Oxford undergraduates to carry out educational work among the poor. Public schools founded missions, to teach young rich boys a social conscience; as Oscar Wilde commented, 'If the lower orders don't set us a good example, what's the use of them?' The Haileybury mission in Stepney converted Clement Attlee to socialism; he later became Mayor and as Prime Minister (1945–51) carried through a social revolution. The process of slum clearance had been accelerated by German bombs, and by the 1950s the population was well below 100,000. It has fallen dramatically since, thanks to the collapse of London's dock industry. St Katharine's Dock, built on the site of a former religious hospital, suppressed at the Reformation, is now a yachting marina, surrounded by luxury flats.

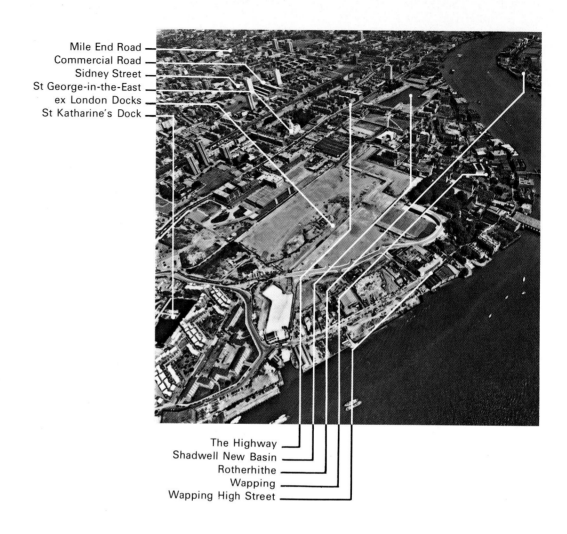

Mile End Road
Commercial Road
Sidney Street
St George-in-the-East
ex London Docks
St Katharine's Dock

The Highway
Shadwell New Basin
Rotherhithe
Wapping
Wapping High Street

WAPPING

The Wapping bend of the river was once a scene of intense commercial life, for the London Docks were the nearest large-size docks to the centre of the city. Among them and to the north of them was a maze of mean streets, occupied not just by dockers but by many immigrant communities. This was an area of intense Jewish settlement, after the Russian pogroms of the 1880s and the 1900s produced panic flights to the West. It was also a nest of revolutionary activity. It was to Sidney Street, in 1911, that Winston Churchill, then Home Secretary, went to supervise efforts by armed police and Scots Guardsmen to subdue a group of Latvian socialist desperadoes holed up in number 100. The 'Siege of Sidney Street' ended with the house burned down, but the Latvians' leader, Peter the Painter, was never found. (His brother later created the Soviet secret police.) The next dramatic art of violence occurred in May 1926, when government efforts to beat the General Strike, by organizing convoys to get food from the docks to the markets, led to the 'Battle of Cable Street'. A decade later, Oswald Mosley led his fascist bands on provocative marches through the Jewish East End, especially in the Mile End Road. The result was the 1936 Public Order Act which banned uniforms and effectively quashed Mosley's movement. Nowadays the docks are dead, filled in and awaiting 'development'; and the old slums have gone, replaced by high-rise council flats. Wapping has lost its violence, its mystery – and its character.

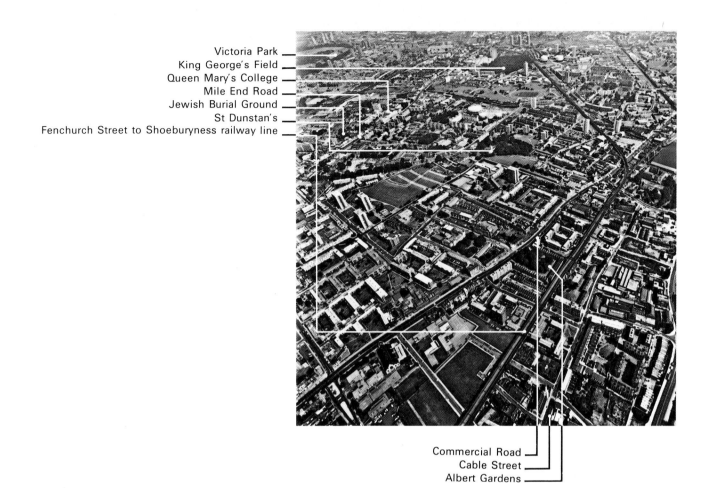

Victoria Park
King George's Field
Queen Mary's College
Mile End Road
Jewish Burial Ground
St Dunstan's
Fenchurch Street to Shoeburyness railway line

Commercial Road
Cable Street
Albert Gardens

SHADWELL

Back in the eighteenth century, Shadwell was a little riverside hamlet. So were Limehouse, Blackwall, Wapping and Ratcliff. Collectively they were known as the Tower hamlets. On this stretch of the river, called the Upper Pool, up to 2,000 ships queued up to get into the available dock-space, and under cover of darkness ruffians from Shadwell and the other hamlets, described as 'River Pirates, Night Plunderers, Light Horsemen, Heavy Horsemen and Mudlarks', would creep aboard to steal. From about 1800 additional docks were built to get cargoes landed more quickly. To accommodate the dockers, mostly Irish and other immigrants, all the riverside hamlets blended into one indistinguishable slum. But a few features emerged

from this wilderness, now replaced by the modern wilderness of council housing and light industry. In the centre is the parish church of Stepney, St Dunstan's, almost the only medieval church of the East End. To the north of it, off the Mile End Road, is the old Jewish Burial Ground (Stepney has some 40 synagogues), and beside it Queen Mary College of the University of London. Next to it is the People's Palace (1885–7), part of the effort to bring enlightened entertainment to this benighted district; and further west still the Whitechapel Art Gallery (1897–9). To the north-east, beyond Bethnal Green, lies Victoria Park, and behind St Dunstan's is the new park of King George's Field.

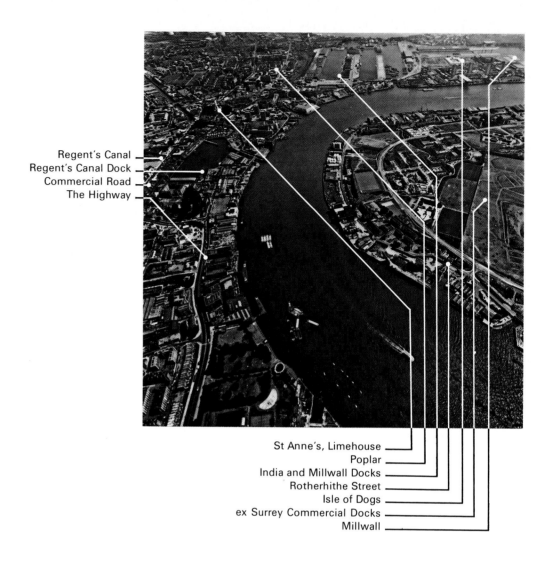

Regent's Canal —
Regent's Canal Dock —
Commercial Road —
The Highway —

St Anne's, Limehouse —
Poplar —
India and Millwall Docks —
Rotherhithe Street —
Isle of Dogs —
ex Surrey Commercial Docks —
Millwall —

REGENT'S CANAL DOCK

London was created by its waterways, not just the Thames but the streams which debouch into it, like the Lea, which wanders through Hackney and Poplar. To these were added man-made water-routes, like the Regent's Canal, which penetrates right into the centre of London, where it links with the Grand Union and so with the canals of the west and Midlands. It strikes the Thames at the Regent's Canal Dock in Limehouse. Here the river meanders in a series of huge loops and bends, the heart of Dockland. To the right of the picture are the old Surrey Commercial Docks in Rotherhithe on the south bank, now mostly filled in. At the top is the huge peninsula called the Isle of Dogs. In the Middle Ages, high walls were built to protect it from the river

tides: in the west the Mill Wall, after the seven windmills which turned there; in the east, the Bleak or Black Wall. Between these walls, from the late seventeenth century onwards, the rich East India Company built its docks. Opposite Poplar and Blackwall, but out of sight in this picture, are Greenwich, and east of it is Woolwich. Beyond Blackwall are the great docks in Silvertown, and further east still are East Ham and Barking. Just beyond the Regent's Canal Dock itself can be seen the superb tower of Hawksmoor's St Anne's, Limehouse (1714–30), one of the first of his East End masterpieces. One sad thing about this fine photograph is that there is not a single ocean-going ship in sight. Until 1914 it was the richest stretch of water in the world.

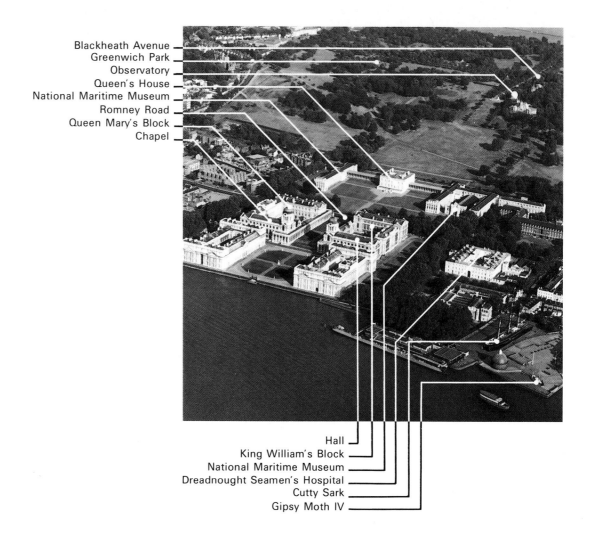

Blackheath Avenue
Greenwich Park
Observatory
Queen's House
National Maritime Museum
Romney Road
Queen Mary's Block
Chapel

Hall
King William's Block
National Maritime Museum
Dreadnought Seamen's Hospital
Cutty Sark
Gipsy Moth IV

GREENWICH

When Henry v's brother, Humphrey Duke of Gloucester, built a river-palace at Greenwich to house his great collection of books (later to form the nucleus of the Bodleian Library in Oxford), he called it 'Bella Vista'. Henry VII embellished it and both his son Henry VIII and his granddaughter, the illustrious Elizabeth, were born there. In 1616 James I added the Queen's House, named after his wife Anne of Denmark, and designed by Inigo Jones as England's first Palladian building. But all fell into decay in the Civil War. So Charles II pulled down the Old Palace, and that eager spirit, John Evelyn the diarist, raised a public subscription to create a retirement hospital for seamen. Wren designed it (using John Webb's plans), assisted by Vanbrugh and Hawksmoor. The Queen's House was refurbished as a residence for the Governor. Up the hill, meanwhile, Charles II had created an observatory, with the first Astronomer Royal housed

beneath a great observation platform, again designed by Wren. Dr Johnson, on a visit, pronounced the hospital 'Too magnificent for charity'. Perhaps, but the old seamen were well housed, clothed and fed, and in 1815 there were 2,710 of them. With Victorian prosperity, numbers fell, and in 1873 the Royal Navy transformed it into a professional training college. In due course the Queen's House became the National Maritime Museum, and when the Astronomer Royal moved to Herstmonceux in Sussex to escape atmospheric pollution, the Observatory became a museum too. Preserved in dry dock are the *Cutty Sark*, once the world's fastest tea-clipper, and *Gipsy Moth IV*, in which Sir Francis Chichester first circumnagivated the world single-handed. The group of buildings forms the finest architectural panorama in England, perhaps in Europe. Bella Vista indeed!

WOOLWICH FLOOD BARRIER

The Woolwich Flood Barrier with its seven movable gates is the centrepiece of London's new flood-control programme launched in 1972, which is costing £500 million. London has always been vulnerable to exceptionally high tides. In 1236 so high was the tide that boatmen were able to take their wherries into Westminster Hall. 'There was last night', wrote Pepys in 1663, 'the greatest tide that ever was remembered in England to have been in this river, all Whitehall having been drowned.' In 1928 flooding killed 14 people in central London, and 300 died in 1953 during floods on the east coast and Thames estuary which might have hit central London too. The risk is growing because not only is London sinking on its clay bed, and all south-east England pivoting down at the rate of a foot per century, but changes have also taken place in the North Sea making sudden surges of high water more severe. Apart from the likely loss of life, a surge-flood in London, it is calculated, could easily do £3,500 million-worth of damage. Downstream of the Barrier, London has built 11.5 miles of new defences, and the entire programme extends from Hounslow and Richmond to Havering and Bexley. The Barrier, opened in 1984, spans the river at a width of 520 metres (570 yards), and in the rest position the gates permit normal traffic to pass. Exceptionally bad conditions can be forecast about 12 hours in advance and it is planned to raise the gates about four hours before the surge-peak. The four main gates are 20 metres (22 yards) high and weigh about 3,700 tonnes; raising time is 30 minutes. When open, each main gate has a clear span of 61 metres (67 yards).

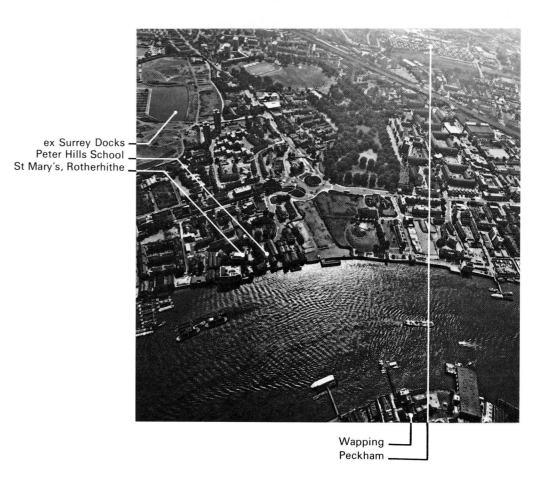

ex Surrey Docks —
Peter Hills School —
St Mary's, Rotherhithe —

Wapping —
Peckham —

ROTHERHITHE

In the eighteenth and nineteenth centuries, Rotherhithe was a pleasant as well as a busy place. This south bank of the Thames, opposite Wapping, was lined with great warehouses, separated by narrow streets leading directly on to the river. But the rich West Indies merchants often lived here too, building themselves fine mansions overlooking the river. In 1714 they pulled down the old medieval parish church of St Mary, Rotherhithe, and commissioned Lancelot Dowbiggin to rebuild it in classical style. Across the churchyard are the fine eighteenth-century premises of what was once the fashion-able Peter Hills School, and near it the engine house for the 1825 Thames Tunnel which runs underneath our picture. Three majestic warehouses remain on this stretch. Many were cleared to extend Southwark Park down to the river. The slums inland have been replaced by council estates. To the east (left in the picture) are the vast wildernesses of the Surrey Docks, now mostly disused and in process of being filled in. Beyond the railway line, which runs from London Bridge Station down into Kent, lie the broad urban acres of south London suburbia.

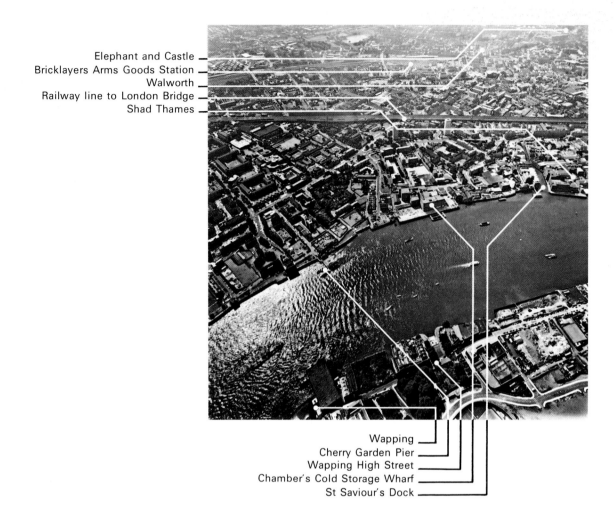

Elephant and Castle
Bricklayers Arms Goods Station
Walworth
Railway line to London Bridge
Shad Thames

Wapping
Cherry Garden Pier
Wapping High Street
Chamber's Cold Storage Wharf
St Saviour's Dock

BERMONDSEY

Bermondsey was once a Cluniac Priory, destroyed at the Reformation, and gradually replaced by an industrial village specializing in leather-work. Street names – Leathermarket Street, Tanner Street, Morocco Street – recall the fact, and the former Leathermarket is on the far right of the picture. The old parish church of St Mary Magdalene, on the far side of the railway from London Bridge, was replaced in Charles II's time. From it, Bermondsey Street meanders under the railway and down to the river. On the right, near Tower Bridge and opposite St Katharine's Dock (both out of the picture) is one of the last genuine industrial areas in London. Shad Thames Street, running alongside the river and the inlet of St Saviour's Dock, still contains many Victorian warehouses and factories, and is criss-crossed by wrought-iron bridges. To the left of St Saviour's Dock was Jacob's Street, containing some of the worst slums in London, replaced between the wars by huge blocks of council flats. Then comes Chamber's Cold Storage Wharf. On the left of the picture all but two of the old wharves have gone, though the Angel Inn remains in solitary dignity over-looking the river. In the middle distance is Bricklayers Arms Goods Station, and beyond it Walworth.

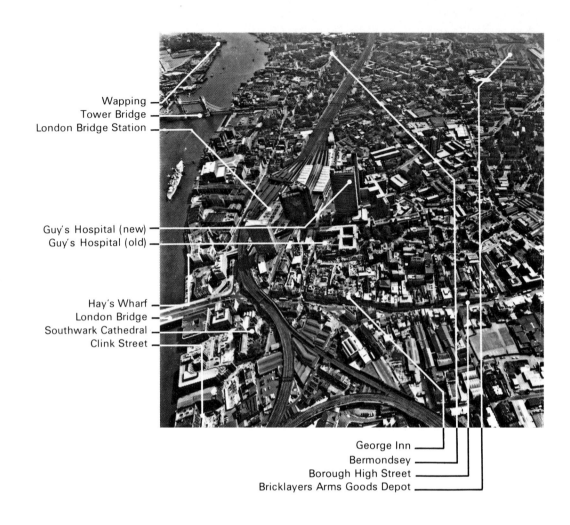

Wapping —
Tower Bridge —
London Bridge Station —

Guy's Hospital (new) —
Guy's Hospital (old) —

Hay's Wharf —
London Bridge —
Southwark Cathedral —
Clink Street —

George Inn —
Bermondsey —
Borough High Street —
Bricklayers Arms Goods Depot —

SOUTHWARK

Apart from the City itself, Southwark is the oldest part of London, because a suburb grew up here in Roman times at the south end of London Bridge. It was 'The Borough', and Borough High Street, leading south, was fringed with famous inns, including the Old Tabard in Talbot Yard, mentioned in Chaucer's *Canterbury Tales*, the White Hart nearby, where Mr Pickwick first met Sam Weller, and the George in King's House Yard, parts of which remain. Dickens knew the Borough well, for his father had been imprisoned for debt in the Marshalsea in Mermaid Court, a setting he used to stunning effect both in *The Pickwick Papers* and *Little Dorrit*. Southwark was notorious for its prisons, including the King's Bench in Scovell Road, which once housed Tobias Smollett, and the Clink in Clink Street. Nearby is Southwark Cathedral, once an Augustinian priory attached to the Bishop of Winchester's palace, one wall of which, with a fine rose window, remains. In medieval times Winchester diocese included the south bank, and the splendid retrochoir of the cathedral was its consistory court. There, under Bloody Mary, Bishop Gardiner, the Lord Chancellor, dispatched heretics to be burned at Smithfield. A generation later, Shakespeare, Ben Jonson and many other south bank dramatists worshipped there. The Borough is crowded with literary memories, for John Keats lived here while he studied medicine at Guy's Hospital (just to the right of London Bridge Station), the great establishment founded by the millionaire stationer Thomas Guy in 1721. Keats's lodging was in Stainer Street, now under the arch of the vast railway network to Cannon Street, Waterloo and Charing Cross Stations.

The Barbican
St Paul's Cathedral
Blackfriars Station
Blackfriars Bridge
King's Reach Tower
Oxo Tower
Upper Ground
London Weekend Television

Stamford Street
Lloyds Computer Centre
Bankside Power Station
Southwark Bridge
London Bridge
Ministry of Transport
Ministry of Defence
Tower Bridge
Blackfriars Road

SHAKESPEARE'S LONDON

The puritanical City fathers had no jurisdiction in the liberties of Southwark, and it was there that Londoners came to have fun, especially to Bankside, the stretch between Southwark and Blackfriars Bridges. First came bear-baiting gardens, to which Bear Gardens and Bear Lane still testify. Then in 1592 Philip Henslowe set up the Rose Theatre in Rose Alley, employing Chapman, Webster, Kyd, Dekker and Drayton as dramatists, and Shakespeare as actor. Three years later the Swan opened in Paris Garden, to the west of Blackfriars Bridge, and in 1599 Richard Burbage transferred his theatre from Shoreditch to Park Street and called it the Globe. Here Shakespeare wrote many of his best plays, including Hamlet, Lear and Macbeth, living next to the Bear Garden, with Beaumont and Fletcher for neighbours. Now the only theatre is the Old Vic on the Waterloo Road. Bankside is given up to the massive bulk of the Bankside Power Station, with its brick tower, and Lloyds Computer Centre. To the west of Blackfriars Bridge, once dominated by the tower of the Oxo Warehouse and its illuminated sign, there are the still more spectacular buildings of the King's Reach development including IPC's 1970s tower, and, in the bottom left of our picture, the great tower of London Weekend Television. As a relief from this twentieth-century gigantism is the Anchor at number 1 Bankside, an eighteenth-century inn from which the brewer Henry Thrale, Dr Johnson's friend, ran his election campaigns, Johnson providing the speeches. The Thrales lived round the corner in Park Street and Johnson had a room in their house.

Law Courts
Fleet Street
New Bridge Street
Blackfriars Station
Unilever House
City of London School
Blackfriars Bridge
Founders Arms

Farringdon Street
Mermaid Theatre
Holborn Viaduct
Smithfield Market
Faraday House
Queen Victoria Street
St Paul's Cathedral
College of Arms

BLACKFRIARS

The old Dominican priory of Blackfriars, just north of where Blackfriars Station now stands, was the scene of one of the most dramatic episodes in English history, in June 1529, when Henry VIII and Catherine of Aragon confronted each other across the Papal legate's court set up to decide whether their marriage was valid. Shakespeare described the event vividly in *Henry VIII*, Act II, Scene 4. Across the road, what is now New Bridge Street, was Henry VIII's Bridewell Palace, which also features in the play. His son Edward VI turned it into a prison, demolished in the 1860s in favour of de Keyser's famous Royal Hotel, itself pulled down (1930) to make way for Unilever House. Next door to it, on Victoria Embankment, is the City of London School, where Prime Minister Asquith was educated. Along Queen Victoria Street, running east from Blackfriars, are many celebrated sites buried beneath modern concrete: Baynard's Castle, which went back to 1100, now occupied by the Mermaid Theatre, the Roman Temple of Mithras, under the huge pile of Bucklersbury

House, and old Doctors' Commons, where Mr Weller Sr bought his disastrous marriage licence in *The Pickwick Papers*, now replaced by the Faraday Building (1932). The ancient town palace of the Earls of Derby, Derby House, was turned into the College of Arms, rebuilt after the fire in brick (1670) and one of the finest seventeenth-century buildings in the City. At that date Blackfriars was still unbridged. Indeed, until the mid-eighteenth century London Bridge was the only permanent crossing below Kingston. Then came Putney Bridge (1729), Westminster (begun in 1738) and in 1760 Robert Mylne's beautiful Blackfriars Bridge. Alas, it decayed and in 1869 was replaced by the present wrought-iron structure with granite piers. Two cast-iron railway bridges of 1862 and 1884 (the western bridge now no longer in use) complete the crossing. On the south bank is the polygonal Founders Arms pub and the jazzy geometry of Southwark council flats.

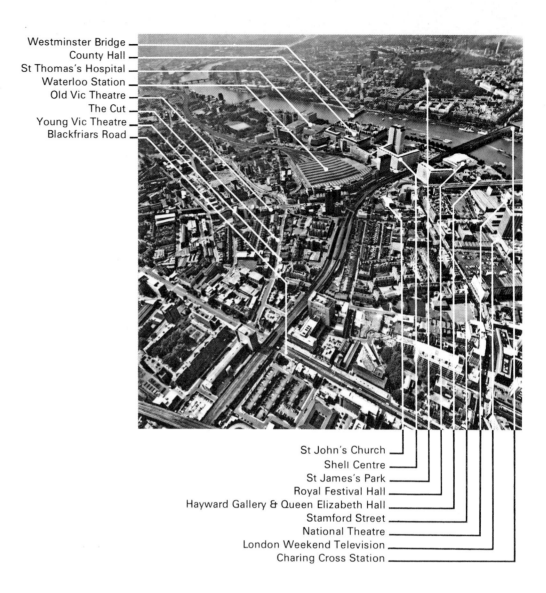

Westminster Bridge —
County Hall —
St Thomas's Hospital —
Waterloo Station —
Old Vic Theatre —
The Cut —
Young Vic Theatre —
Blackfriars Road —

St John's Church —
Shell Centre —
St James's Park —
Royal Festival Hall —
Hayward Gallery & Queen Elizabeth Hall —
Stamford Street —
National Theatre —
London Weekend Television —
Charing Cross Station —

WATERLOO

The great bends and loops in the Thames tend to confuse and disorientate. The top of this picture is the west, the bottom the south. The main railway line running diagonally across it leads from Charing Cross Station, in front of Waterloo, in the direction of London Bridge, crossing over Blackfriars Road and under the line south to Elephant and Castle. London has been trying to redevelop this scruffy area for the best part of a century, and with indifferent success. In the years 1900–20 Waterloo, the country's biggest station, was erected with a tremendously grand façade by J.R. Scott. But the main frontal view from the splendid St John's Church (1822) opposite, is obscured by the hideous railway viaduct of the Charing Cross line. Then, over fifty years beginning in 1908, came the vast complex known as County Hall, from which London is governed. Ralph Knott's design looks magnificent from the river side, but from the south it is obscured by its own

protecting wings, built, after his death, from 1935. The complicated cultural centre on the South Bank, built since the war between the Hungerford Railway Bridge and Blackfriars, was equally ambitious. The Royal Festival Hall (1948–51) was the first 'modern' public building in Britain; the National Film Theatre (1956–8), the Hayward Gallery-Queen Elizabeth Hall group (1965–8) and the National Theatre (1961–76) were all fashionable in their day. But they are completely overshadowed by the Shell Centre (1953–63), some parts of which are 26 storeys, with the tower reaching a height of 338 feet. The whole is faced in Portland stone, England's best building material, and this, together with the granite of County Hall, make the concrete of the cultural centre look dingy. This great group of buildings look impressive from afar – that is, from the north bank – but at close quarters they are charmless.

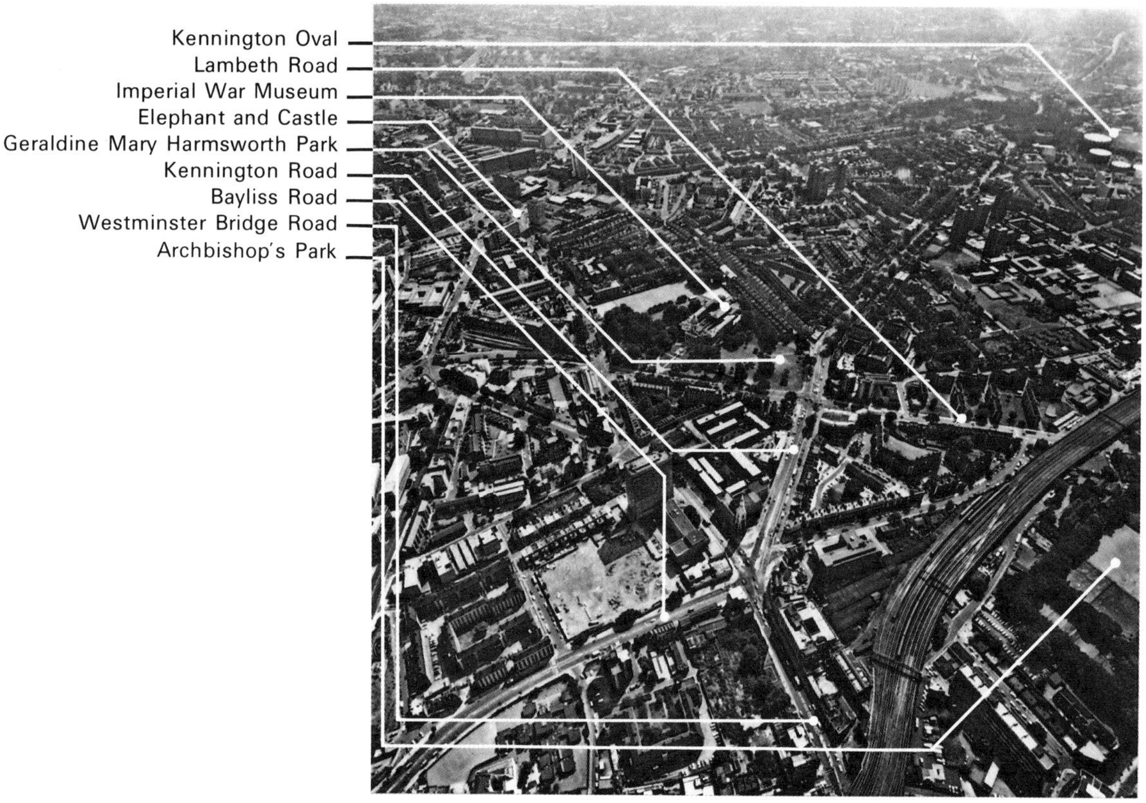

Kennington Oval —
Lambeth Road —
Imperial War Museum —
Elephant and Castle —
Geraldine Mary Harmsworth Park —
Kennington Road —
Bayliss Road —
Westminster Bridge Road —
Archbishop's Park —

LAMBETH

In this picture the great medieval parish of Southwark merges into another vast parish, Lambeth. It was dominated by two dignitaries. One was the Archbishop of Canterbury, the beginning of whose Lambeth Palace Park can be seen on the right. Just beyond it is Kennington, which Edward III gave to his infant son, Edward. He grew up to be a mighty warrior and is commemorated by Black Prince Road, which runs alongside the remains of his palace. The lands are still attached to the Duchy of Cornwall, the personal property of the heir to the throne, so the ground-rents of the pleasant houses in and off Kennington Lane keep the present Prince of Wales in the style to which he is accustomed. The district is also famous for the Oval (1846), headquarters of Surrey County Cricket Club, dominated by Jack Hobbs (active 1903–34), England's greatest batsman. Left of the

great band of railway lines coming out of Waterloo Station is Geraldine Mary Harmsworth Park, which commemorates the adored mother of the newspaper tycoon, Northcliffe, and in it is the Imperial War Museum by James Lewis (1812). For a century it housed the inmates of the Royal Bethlehem Hospital for the Care of the Insane, known as Bedlam. The real bedlam today is down St George's Road at the Elephant and Castle. This district, and St George's Circus below it, have always been a muddled confluence of roads and radicals. Wilkes assembled his mobs here; so did the Gordon Rioters. An eighteenth-century attempt by Robert Mylne to replan the roads did not work, and the London authorities had another go in the 1950s. The result is one of the worst bits of urban planning in the metropolis, a nightmare of tunnels for the pedestrian and confusion for the motorist.

Home Park Road —
Wimbledon Park Lake —
Wimbledon Park —
All England Lawn Tennis Club —
Church Road —

WIMBLEDON

When William Cecil, the great Lord Burghley, leased Wimbledon Manor from the Crown in the 1550s, the only form of tennis known to humanity was royal or 'real' tennis, played notably at Henry VIII's splendid courts at Hampton Court and Whitehall. Cecil's son Thomas carved out a park from the wilderness of Wimbledon Common and built a fine house on Home Park Road. It was later owned and rebuilt by Queen Henrietta Maria, Sarah Duchess of Marlborough, the Pembrokes and the Spencers. Nothing now remains of it. But the open spaces remained open, the Common being the best bit of real country in the entire London area, and famous for duelling. In 1840 the Earl of Cardigan, who later commanded the Charge of the Light Brigade, fought the last duel in England here, wounding his man and then standing trial for attempted murder in the House of Lords. Queen Victoria, shocked, later encouraged legal, if still martial, use of the wilderness: from 1860 the new Territorials assembled here and held shooting matches; the district became sporty. So in 1868 a group of croquet fanatics bought the old park to establish the All England Croquet Club and hold national championships. The same year, as it happened, a Major Gem had marked out a court for the new middle-class game of lawn tennis. When tennis enthusiasts wanted to play championships at Lord's, the all-male MCC refused, as women were already keen on tennis. So tennis moved to the Wimbledon Croquet Club, which had admitted women from the start, and soon took it over. The first championships were held in 1877, and since the present ground was built in 1922 the Wimbledon fortnight has remained the most glittering event of any sport.

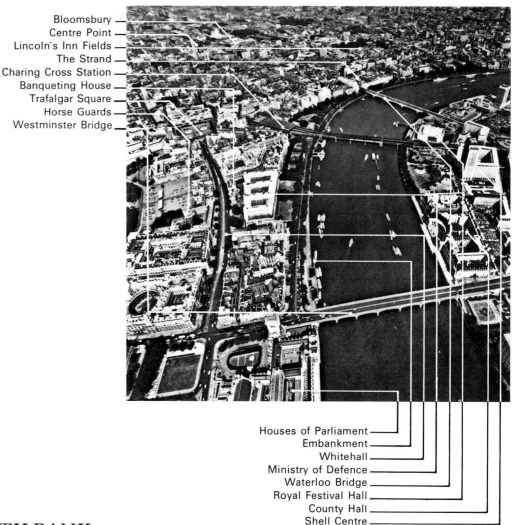

Bloomsbury
Centre Point
Lincoln's Inn Fields
The Strand
Charing Cross Station
Banqueting House
Trafalgar Square
Horse Guards
Westminster Bridge

Houses of Parliament
Embankment
Whitehall
Ministry of Defence
Waterloo Bridge
Royal Festival Hall
County Hall
Shell Centre

WHITEHALL AND THE SOUTH BANK

Here we have the whole panorama of central west London, both north and south of the river. To the right, straddling Waterloo Bridge, is the South Bank cultural complex, and below it the vast Shell building and the spread of County Hall. On the north bank we can trace the movement of London westwards. The City ended at Temple Bar, which divided Fleet Street from the Strand, the ancient road which led to the quite separate borough of Westminster. This once ended at Westminster Bridge in the foreground. The stretch of river bank in between was slowly settled, in the late Middle Ages, by great ecclesiastical and secular lords, who built their town houses there, with gardens stretching down to the river along which they moved in their state barges: Arundel House, Essex House, Somerset House, John of Gaunt's great Lancastrian palace of the Savoy, above all York House, the property of the Archbishop of York. Here Cardinal Wolsey built himself a splendid house, York Place, and when Henry VIII broke him

in 1529 he seized it (along with Hampton Court) and converted it into his main London palace, now called Whitehall, for his Westminster Palace had already become a centre of administration and parliament. Whitehall Palace gradually covered a vast area, on both sides of the street, with the tennis courts, cockpit and tiltyard on the left and the main royal apartments on the right overlooking the river. The two halves were linked by the Holbein Gate, near the Banqueting House which Inigo Jones built for James I, and the King's Gate off Parliament Square. Nothing now remains except Henry VIII's wine-cellar in the foundation of the Ministry of Defence's vast quadragon. The tiltyard, tennis courts and cockpit were cleared by Charles II to make Horse Guards Parade. The rest of the palace – except the Banqueting Hall – burned down in the 1690s, so royalty left Whitehall for good. Over the next 200 years, civil servants made Whitehall their own village.

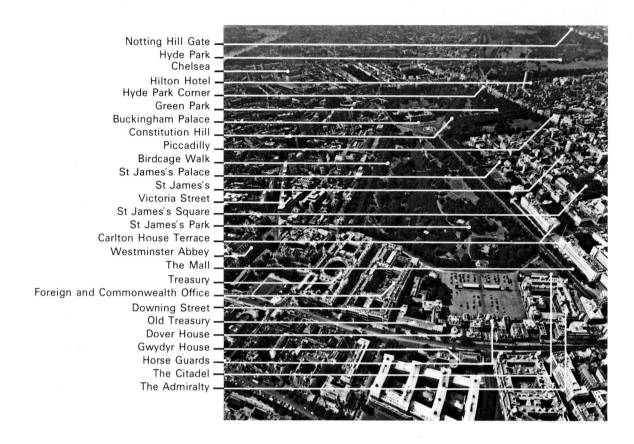

Notting Hill Gate
Hyde Park
Chelsea
Hilton Hotel
Hyde Park Corner
Green Park
Buckingham Palace
Constitution Hill
Piccadilly
Birdcage Walk
St James's Palace
St James's
Victoria Street
St James's Square
St James's Park
Carlton House Terrace
Westminster Abbey
The Mall
Treasury
Foreign and Commonwealth Office
Downing Street
Old Treasury
Dover House
Gwydyr House
Horse Guards
The Citadel
The Admiralty

THE LUNGS OF LONDON

This picture covers most of London's West End, with Chelsea in the far distance, and it gives a good idea of Henry VIII's gigantic impact on the capital. Until his reign, most of this area was Church land and nearly all agricultural. As we have seen, he acquired York Place and its gardens (quite illegally) and built Whitehall there. But when he nationalized the monasteries by Acts of Parliament, later in the 1530s, he carried through two major concentrations of abbey lands. He enclosed 630 acres as a deer park, later to be called Hyde Park, and he brought together a further 180 acres, stretching from Charing Cross on the right of the picture down into Westminster, and with the present Hyde Park Corner as its apex. Much of this was marshland, which he drained. In the centre of it he built what was then regarded as a country place, St James's Palace. Its gardens gradually evolved into St James's Park itself, Green Park and the gardens of Buckingham Palace. Thus Henry VIII's depredations created a belt of green in the western heart of London. These royal possessions were not very private. In Whitehall the main London–Westminster road ran right through the middle of the palace area. Londoners could attend outdoor sermons within the palace precincts and, if suitably dressed, could walk in the main garden. Charles II opened St James's Park to the public in the 1660s, by which time, one imagines, the two crocodiles put in the lake by James I had died. People have been admitted to the present Hyde Park since Charles I's day, though when Whitehall burned down in the 1690s, a hundred acres or so were lopped off it to make Kensington Palace. Today an energetic Londoner can walk over ten miles from Westminster to Notting Hill Gate (in the top right-hand corner) and only twice set foot on a road.

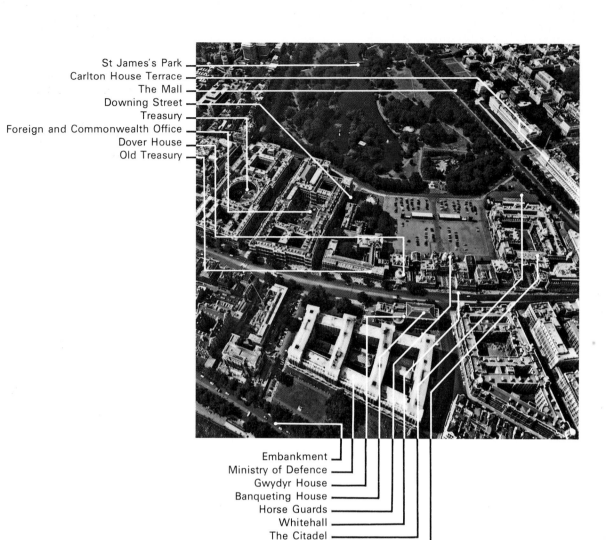

St James's Park
Carlton House Terrace
The Mall
Downing Street
Treasury
Foreign and Commonwealth Office
Dover House
Old Treasury

Embankment
Ministry of Defence
Gwydyr House
Banqueting House
Horse Guards
Whitehall
The Citadel
The Admiralty

CIVIL SERVANTS' LONDON

Here we have the heart of British government, from which (until the late 1940s) a quarter of the earth's surface was administered. Present-day Whitehall is essentially a creation of the eighteenth and nineteenth centuries. From right to left, we have have first the Admiralty, built 1722–6 by Thomas Ripley, with a big late-Victorian addition beyond it and, overlooking St James's Park, a monstrous World War Two fortress called the Citadel, which authority is always meaning to pull down but never does. The finest bit is Admiralty House, built by S.P. Cockerell in the 1780s and reckoned the best ministerial home of the lot. The Admiralty itself has a screen by Robert Adam. Next is William Kent's Horse Guards (1740s), with the parade ground used for Trooping the Colour beyond it. For 300 years it was Army HQ, but is now merged in the vast Ministry of Defence (below the Banqueting House) first designed in 1913 but not completed till 1959. Next to the Horse Guards is domed Dover House, the prettiest building in

Whitehall, designed by Henry Holland in the 1780s and now the Scottish Office. Wales is run from Gwydyr House (1770s) opposite. Then comes the Old Treasury (now the Cabinet Offices), built in bits over a century by everyone from Kent to Barry. Behind it is Downing Street, put up as speculative housing by Sir George Downing in the 1680s, but the home of the Prime Minister and the Chancellor of the Exchequer since the days of Sir Robert Walpole. It is much bigger than it looks from the front and there is an awful lot more underground. Across Downing Street is the vast government complex housing the Home Office (front) and the Foreign and Commonwealth Office (back). This was designed by Sir George Gilbert Scott in 1861 in the Italian style on the instructions of Lord Palmerston, who hated Gothic. Across King Charles Street is J.M. Brydon's late-Victorian block which now houses the Treasury and much else. Below ground, at the park end, is Churchill's wartime bunker.

Vauxhall Bridge
Vincent Square
Tate Gallery
Westminster Cathedral
Millbank
Department of the Environment
Lambeth Bridge
Victoria Street
Victoria Tower Gardens
Lambeth Palace
Victoria Tower
Westminster Hall
Clock Tower ('Big Ben')
Westminster Bridge
St Thomas's Hospital

Westminster Abbey
Parliament Square
ex Scotland Yard

THE HOUSES OF PARLIAMENT

The Anglo-Saxon kings transferred their principal capital from Winchester to Thorney Island, west of London, early in the eleventh century. They endowed a monastery there and Edward the Confessor built a great basilica, soon called Westminster Abbey. Across the road from the church was the palace, embellished by William Rufus in the 1090s with a vast hall, which Richard II crowned with the finest hammer-beam roof in Europe. It is all that remains of the original palace. Just south of the palace was the royal chapel of St Stephen's, built by Henry III in imitation of Louis IX's Sainte-Chapelle in Paris. When the House of Commons emerged in the fourteenth century, St Stephen's became its home, and remained so until virtually the whole of Westminster Palace was burned down in 1834. The contract to rebuild parliament was awarded to Charles Barry, designer of the Travellers' and Reform Clubs. In 1835 he said he could do it in six years. In fact it took the last 25 years of his life, for MPs constantly interfered, and before he could even begin he had to build a coffer dam and lay down thousands of tons of concrete, for Westminster is built on quicksand. At the west end he put up what was then the world's tallest skyscraper, the Victoria Tower; at the east the famous clock tower, with its mechanism by Dent's and its great bell, Big Ben, called after the Commissioner of Works, Sir Benjamin Hall. Parliament was badly damaged by bombs in 1941 but later restored to its original condition. The recent cleaning has revealed it as Britain's greatest exercise in Gothic Revival – some would say the finest of all our nineteenth-century buildings.

Department of the Environment
Victoria Street
Westminster Abbey
Parliament Square
Victoria Tower
Westminster Hall
Clock Tower ('Big Ben')

WESTMINSTER ABBEY

Westminster Abbey is the world's outstanding example of a state church. Except briefly during the decade 1540–50 it has never been a bishop's seat, though it is used for many cathedral functions. It is the ceremonial church of royalty and in terms of ecclesiastical structure is a 'Royal Peculiar'. Hence it is perhaps the only church in England whose entire fabric has liturgical purposes, for even the gallery was designed to be used at coronations (as it still is). Edward the Confessor richly endowed the Abbey and built a glorious Romanesque church for it. His body lies amid the royal tombs in the choir, and the plan of his church dictated the outline of the present structure. From 1245 on, however, Henry III began to rebuild it. He made it the most 'French' of great English churches, giving it the highest nave (102 feet) in England, though its great length, following the Confessor's ground plan, is characteristically English. French, too, is the cluster of semicircular chapels at the east end, though here also, early in the sixteenth century, the middle one was replaced by the spectacular Henry VII Chapel, an exercise in ultra-English Late Perpendicular. Both Henry Yevele, the greatest English medieval architect, and Christopher Wren, our greatest baroque one, worked on the church; and the gentlemanly west towers were put up by Nicholas Hawksmoor as late as 1735–40. The main entrance is through the north transept, whose front was reconstructed by J.L. Pearson with Sir George Gilbert Scott in the mid-nineteenth century. Thus the Abbey has been created over nine centuries by many of England's finest architects: 'Like some tall palm, the noiseless fabric sprang', as Sir Walter Scott put it. The contribution of the present age has been to clean it, so we can now grasp both its noble structure and the brilliance of its sculptural detail.

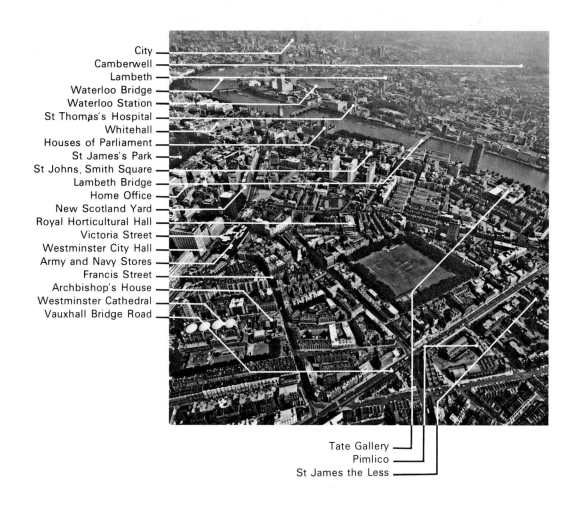

City —
Camberwell —
Lambeth —
Waterloo Bridge —
Waterloo Station —
St Thomas's Hospital —
Whitehall —
Houses of Parliament —
St James's Park —
St Johns, Smith Square —
Lambeth Bridge —
Home Office —
New Scotland Yard —
Royal Horticultural Hall —
Victoria Street —
Westminster City Hall —
Army and Navy Stores —
Francis Street —
Archbishop's House —
Westminster Cathedral —
Vauxhall Bridge Road —

Tate Gallery —
Pimlico —
St James the Less —

WHERE CHURCH AND STATE MEET

To the south-west of the Abbey and the Houses of Parliament lies much of the central administrative area of church and state. Thus in Dean's Yard is Sir Herbert Baker's Church House (1937–40), from which the Church of England is governed, though the Archbishopric of Canterbury is run from Lambeth Palace, just across the river to the east of Lambeth Bridge. The Methodists have their Central Hall (1905–11), with its Frenchified dome, in Storey's Gate, the Catholics their cathedral and Archbishop's House off Victoria Street. Since the Second World War central government has sprawled into this region. Along Victoria Street is the new Department of Trade and Industry (early 1960s), New Scotland Yard (mid-1960s) and beyond them, overlooking St James's Park, the grotesque new premises of the Home Office. There are also three harsh slabs, 200 feet high and containing 3,600 civil servants, off Marsham Street. But fortunate people live around here too, especially in the seventeenth- and eighteenth-century houses between Birdcage Walk and Horseferry Road. This is known as the Division Bell Area, because MPs with houses or flats here have division bells installed which enable them to scuttle to the lobbies in the vital ten minutes before the vote is taken. Dominating this area used to be St John's, Smith Square, the grandiose four-towered church built by Thomas Archer in 1714–28; gutted during the war, it is now a concert hall. To the south and west of Westminster School playing fields, in the centre of the picture, were once some of the worst slums in London. Vauxhall Bridge Road in 1816 and Victoria Street in the 1850s were driven through them to improve the area, and the Anglicans launched their own programme of slum evangelism by building three fine churches: Benjamin Ferrey's St Stephen's, off Vincent Square, Scott's St Matthew's, Great Peter Street (gutted by fire a few years ago), and, on Vauxhall Bridge Road itself, G.E. Street's magnificent St James-the-Less.

WESTMINSTER CATHEDRAL

In the last quarter of the nineteenth century, under Cardinal Manning, the Roman Catholic Church in England flourished, and some of its stalwarts even thought all England would be 'converted'. So the new cathedral at Westminster was to be magnificent. The commission was awarded in 1894 to J.F. Bentley, a famous designer of fonts and altarpieces. Hitherto, since the Anglicans built in Gothic, the Catholics had always opted for Roman baroque. Bentley toured Venice and Ravenna, and the design he produced might be called Italian Byzantine. The clergy said they must have a long nave in the English fashion, so Bentley lined up four domes in a row, calling the last the chancel, added a half-dome apse at the east end, and a Venetian campanile tower at the west. He designed the cathedral from the top downwards, and from the outside inwards, adding a superlative west front composed of a giant Italianate porch surmounted by a receding series of domes. Bentley was a master of detail, colour and surface glitter, and he made skilful use of contrasting brick and white stone. Now that the cathedral has been cleaned, the old clutter to the west of it swept away, and its red-and-white pavemented approach-piazza finished, it makes one of the most dramatic polychrome buildings in London. Alas, the interior, planned by Bentley to be a dazzling Aladdin's cave of marble surfaces up to 30 feet, and above that colour-and-gilt mosaic pictures, has never been finished (except in the Lady Chapel). For the steam went out of the Catholic Revival and most of the inside remains bare, dark brick. The work is best seen from the outside, where its originality still astonishes.

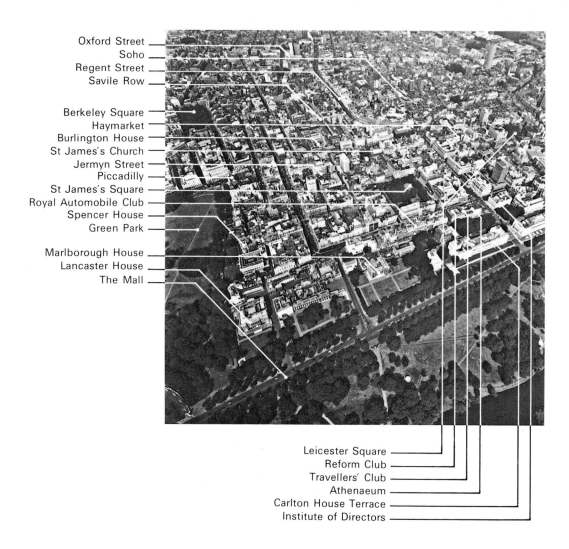

Oxford Street
Soho
Regent Street
Savile Row

Berkeley Square
Haymarket
Burlington House
St James's Church
Jermyn Street
Piccadilly
St James's Square
Royal Automobile Club
Spencer House
Green Park

Marlborough House
Lancaster House
The Mall

Leicester Square
Reform Club
Travellers' Club
Athenaeum
Carlton House Terrace
Institute of Directors

CLUBMAN'S LONDON

St James's, the 150 acres bounded by The Mall to the south, Green Park to the west, Piccadilly to the north and the Haymarket to the east, has long been the most socially desirable and financially valuable address in London. Henry VIII built the palace in the 1530s but it was not until after the Restoration, in the 1660s, that Henry Jermyn, Lord St Albans, began to build St James's Square, the third square in London (after Covent Garden and Lincoln's Inn Fields) and the first in the West End. In the 1670s he got Wren to put up the magnificent St James's Church in Piccadilly, and thirty years later Wren adorned the south side of the district with Marlborough House, built for the great Duke on Crown land. All this south side belongs to Crown or state, for west of the palace is Lancaster House (1825) by Benjamin Wyatt, once leased to the multi-millionaire first Duke of Sutherland, later the home of George V and now the scene of big government shindigs. East of Marlborough House was old Carlton House, much beautified by the spendthrift George IV, then (1827) pulled down and replaced by

Nash's superb Carlton House Terrace. Of the grand houses once lived in by the nobility, only Vardy's Spencer House (1750s) on St James's Place, is left in private hands. But St James's is still clubman's London, though Nash's United Services, on Waterloo Place, is now the Institute of Directors. Opposite, the Athenaeum (1828) by Decimus Burton survives, and other clubs on Pall Mall are Barry's Travellers' (1829) and the Reform (1837), the Oxford and Cambridge (1835) by the brothers Smirke, and the Edwardian Royal Automobile Club. In St James's Street itself are (on the left) the Devonshire (1827) by Benjamin Wyatt, Brooks's (1777) by Holland, the Carlton (1826) by Hopper and (on the right) White's (1787) by James Wyatt and Boodles (1775) by J. Crunden. Clubmen buy their boots and hats at Lobb's and Lock's at the bottom of the street, their shirts in Jermyn Street, and their suits in Savile Row, across Piccadilly at the back of Burlington House.

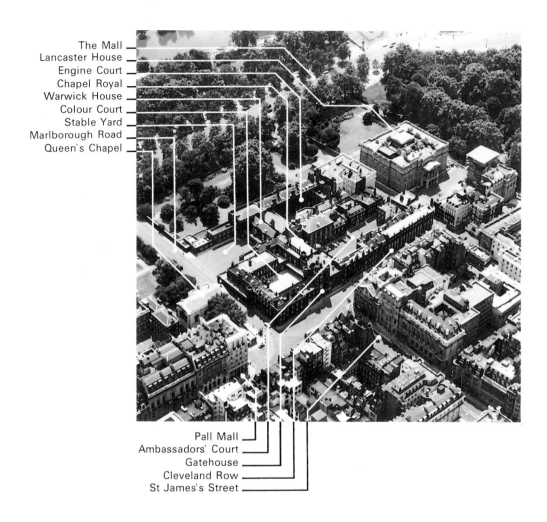

The Mall
Lancaster House
Engine Court
Chapel Royal
Warwick House
Colour Court
Stable Yard
Marlborough Road
Queen's Chapel

Pall Mall
Ambassadors' Court
Gatehouse
Cleveland Row
St James's Street

ST JAMES'S PALACE

The Manor of St James was marshland belonging to Eton College until Henry VIII decided to build a country palace there for Anne Boleyn. He enclosed a park and filled it with deer, draining the marsh in the process. But the site remained malarial, and as recently as the 1890s the future George V, who lived in the section of it called York House, declared: 'This is a beastly house and I think very unhealthy.' The palace itself, of brick and fine Caen stone, with delicate plaster-of-Paris ceilings, is handsome but had an unlucky reputation. Boleyn herself had it for only two years before her execution; then Henry gave it to his illegitimate son, the Duke of Richmond, who promptly died there. Its next tenant, Thomas Cromwell, went to the scaffold. Queen Mary died there of a fever, possibly malaria. Elizabeth used it only when Whitehall was being cleaned, and James I never – giving it instead to his adored heir Prince Henry, who died there aged eighteen. Charles I was taken there as a prisoner in 1648, and the next year walked across the park to his execution outside the Banqueting House.

In Charles II's time both he and his brother used it to accommodate their mistresses, equipping it with a mass-chapel for the Catholic ones, such as the Duchesse de Mazarin, whose shade provides the palace ghost. But after he became king, James II installed his wife, Mary of Modena, in the palace and in 1688 she gave birth to the Old Pretender, the so-called 'baby in a warming pan' which provoked the Glorious Revolution. Here, in 1712, Queen Anne touched the stripling Dr Johnson for the 'King's Evil' (scrofula) and in 1737 occurred the death of Queen Caroline, so vividly described in Hervey's memoirs. George III survived three assassination attempts in the palace, and it was here in 1812 that his dreadful son the Duke of Cumberland murdered his valet, Sellis, by slitting his throat. The traditional royal receptions or levées ended in 1939 but twenty or so senior royal servants still have apartments there, and all ambassadors are accredited to 'the Court of St James'.

The Mall —
Buckingham Palace —
Piccadilly —
Green Park —
Mayfair —
Grosvenor Place —
St Peter's, Eaton Square —
Hyde Park Corner —

Elizabeth Street —
St Michael's, Chester Square —
Victoria Station —
Buckingham Palace Road —

BELGRAVIA

When Henry VIII dissolved the Abbey of Westminster not all its west London estates remained in royal hands. By the mid-seventeenth century about 300 acres of them, stretching from what is now Bond Street almost to Millbank on the Thames, had fallen into the hands of Hugh Audley, a moneylender, who died in 1662. They eventually passed to his great-grand-niece Mary Davies. She married, as a child-bride of thirteen, a rich Cheshire baronet, Sir Thomas Grosvenor, and their heir, Sir Richard, developed Mayfair in the first two decades of the eighteenth century. A century later, however, the Grosvenor lands south of Hyde Park Corner were still fields and market gardens. In 1821 Thomas Cundy became surveyor of the Grosvenor estate and began to implement James Wyatt's plan to turn the fields into a series of elegant streets, squares and crescents, which would form a new aristocratic quarter to rival Mayfair but with bigger houses and larger gardens. He brought together a number of contractors, the chief of whom was the great self-made builder Thomas Cubitt. Cubitt had already developed Highbury, parts of Bloomsbury and St Pancras, and was laying out the south London suburb of Clapham. Between 1825 and his death in 1855 he built hundreds of magnificent houses in the district enclosed by Grosvenor Place, Buckingham Palace Road, Wilton Crescent and Elizabeth Street. Cundy's son Thomas supplied the area with churches, completed in 1846, such as St Michael's, Chester Square though the dominant church in the area, St Peter's, Eaton Square (1824), was by Henry Hakewell. The area was known as Belgravia by the 1840s and virtually all the street names reflect Grosvenor connections. Meanwhile, as their rent-roll increased, the family ascended the peerage. Mayfair brought them a barony (1761) and an earldom (1784); Belgravia added a marquisate (1831) and the Dukedom of Westminster in 1874.

64

The Mall
St James's Park
Birdcage Walk
Buckingham Palace Road
Queen Victoria Memorial

BUCKINGHAM PALACE

In the past the royal family were not lucky with their London homes. The Tower and Bridewell Palace were too smelly, Westminster and Whitehall Palaces burnt down, St James's was too small and unhealthy, Kensington too remote. The site now occupied by Buckingham Palace, which includes a 40-acre garden and a 5-acre lake, was part of the Eton College estate acquired by Henry VIII. He turned it into a garden. James I planted mulberry trees in a commercial venture to produce silk, and Mulberry Garden later became a public resort, like Ranelagh or Vauxhall. Successive houses were built by Lord Gording, the Earl of Arlington and the Duke of Buckingham, and then in 1762 it was bought by George III and called Queen's House after his wife Charlotte. Other names were Pimlico Palace and St George's Palace. George III used it chiefly to house his great library, now in the British Museum. His heir George IV got Nash to rebuild it completely, and

alterations by Pennethorne continued under William IV until his death. So Victoria was the first monarch actually to live in it, and she made it what it is, a very grand, rather dull state house. She shifted Nash's Marble Arch entrance to the site of the old hanging place of Tyburn. In the years before the First World War Sir Aston Webb designed a huge circus in front of the palace to provide a triumphant culmination to The Mall, and at the same time he gave the palace itself a new façade. For a century up to the 1960s debutantes were presented at the palace, one of them, a suffragette, telling George V in June 1914, 'For God's sake, Your Majesty, stop torturing women'. Garden parties continue, however, on the vast lawn in the bottom half of the picture, and until the Second World War the Royal Watermen, in scarlet and brass, rowed guests up and down the lake.

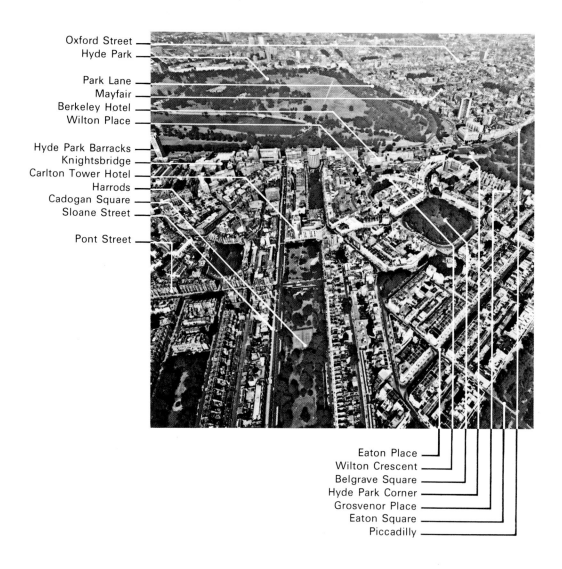

Oxford Street
Hyde Park

Park Lane
Mayfair
Berkeley Hotel
Wilton Place

Hyde Park Barracks
Knightsbridge
Carlton Tower Hotel
Harrods
Cadogan Square
Sloane Street

Pont Street

Eaton Place
Wilton Crescent
Belgrave Square
Hyde Park Corner
Grosvenor Place
Eaton Square
Piccadilly

DEBUTANTES' LONDON

Here is old-fashioned debutantes' London, with Belgravia merging into Knightsbridge and the Grosvenor estate into the Cadogan estate. The 'season' was an invention of the first half of the nineteenth century, and lasted until the 1960s. During its heyday it began with the Royal Academy Dinner in the late spring, and ended after the Goodwood race-meeting in July. There was also a Little Season in November and December. These periods originally coincided with parliamentary sittings. Up till 1914 debland was Wilton Place and Wilton Crescent, taking in Belgrave Square, Eaton Place and Eaton Square, and the streets that bisect them (plus Mayfair of course). Cadogan Place and Cadogan Square were passable, but Pont Street was dowdy. Today, scarcely any of the big Belgravia houses are owned by individuals. Embassies have taken over (for example, the Mexican at the north-east corner of Belgrave Square, the Spanish at the south-

east corner, and the French on Knightsbridge next to the Hyde Park Hotel (1888). Debs have become Sloane Rangers and pushed out of the picture to the bottom end of Sloane Street and beyond in the King's Road area, though some still lurk on the Cadogan estates. Office blocks and national headquarters abound: in Grosvenor Place the British Steel Corporation (1956) and General Accident (1958), and the National Farmers Union on Knightsbridge. Knightsbridge, or King's Bridge, the old main road to the west, has been cleared of private houses, and endowed with new luxury hotels: the Berkeley (1965) shifted from Mayfair, the round tower of the London Park Tower (1971), and the Carlton Tower at the top end of Cadogan Place. The 1960s skyscraper of the Hyde Park Barracks, which houses the Household Cavalry ('The Tins'), still provides remaining debs with escorts.

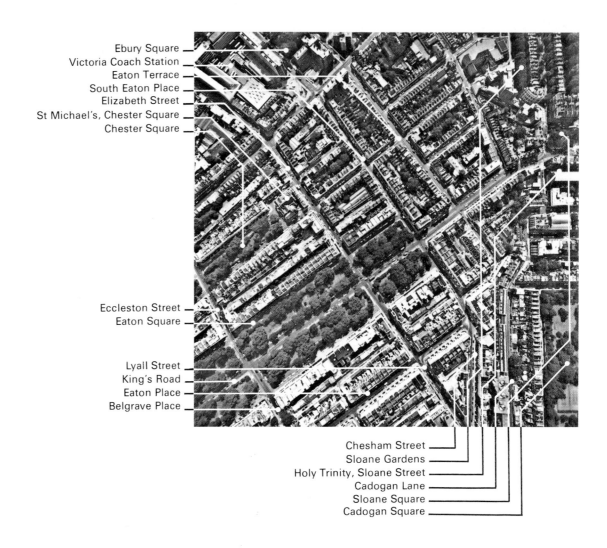

Ebury Square
Victoria Coach Station
Eaton Terrace
South Eaton Place
Elizabeth Street
St Michael's, Chester Square
Chester Square

Eccleston Street
Eaton Square

Lyall Street
King's Road
Eaton Place
Belgrave Place

Chesham Street
Sloane Gardens
Holy Trinity, Sloane Street
Cadogan Lane
Sloane Square
Cadogan Square

EATON SQUARE

Eaton Square, called after the famous Cheshire estate of the Grosvenors, is still perhaps London's grandest address. It is not a square at all, but an elongated oblong, bisected moreover by a busy main road, the section of the King's Road (originally a private royal road) running from Buckingham Palace to Sloane Square. Until 1939 many of these enormous houses were occupied by individual families, among them for instance Britain's last great diarist, Sir Henry ('Chips') Channon MP, who lived there with the Duke of Kent on one side of him and Lord ('Rab') Butler on the other. One Tory MP, Julian Amery, still has a whole house on the square, and part of number one remains the home of the doyen of parliamentarians, Lord Boothby. Nearly all the houses are now divided into flats, duplexes and penthouses, as the variations in the roofscape testify. Thomas Cubitt, who built much of the square, believed in varying the pattern, but it is the alterations of recent years which have produced the patchwork-quilt effect. Eaton Square is grand and formal; Chester Square, above it, is much cosier, with its charming church of St Michael by Thomas Cundy (1846) providing a parish note. The outstanding church of the district is Holy Trinity, at the bottom of Sloane Street almost overlooking Sloane Square. It was designed by J.D. Sedding at the end of the 1880s in what is known as the Arts and Crafts style, with many brilliant decorative features including stained glass by Sir Edward Burne-Jones. It is generally reckoned to be one of London's finest Anglican churches, as befits this neighbourhood.

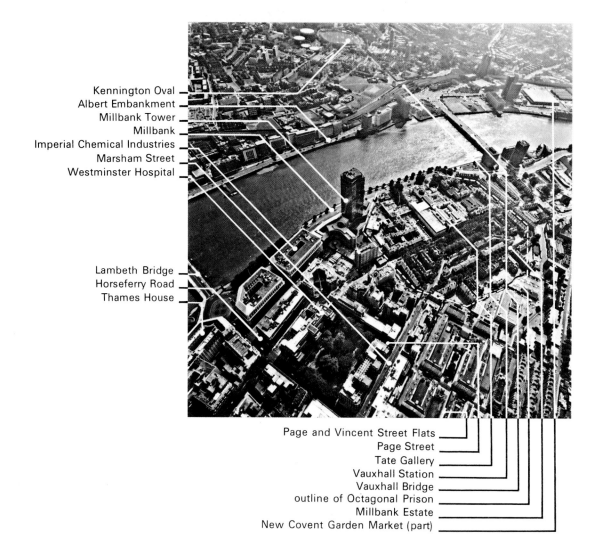

Kennington Oval
Albert Embankment
Millbank Tower
Millbank
Imperial Chemical Industries
Marsham Street
Westminster Hospital

Lambeth Bridge
Horseferry Road
Thames House

Page and Vincent Street Flats
Page Street
Tate Gallery
Vauxhall Station
Vauxhall Bridge
outline of Octagonal Prison
Millbank Estate
New Covent Garden Market (part)

MILLBANK

Like everything else to do with Westminster, Millbank had its origins in the old Abbey estate. Here was the monks' chief water-mill, on the bank of the Thames, later used to provide the district's water supply. Now this pretty stretch of the river between Lambeth and Vauxhall Bridges is without much unifying character. On the south bank the far horizon is filled in by Kennington and its Oval cricket ground, while the stretch near the river once occupied by London's great pleasure gardens of Vauxhall is carved up into office blocks whose lack of symmetry or pattern provides a mediocre skyline. The north bank, though more imposing, is not much better. Imperial Chemical Industries and Thames House, to the right of Lambeth Bridge, are dull examples of interwar neo-classicism, while next to them the Vickers Building, with its 32-storey glass tower rising to nearly 390 feet, is a typical exercise in early Sixties modernism. The Tate Gallery (1897), which incongruously houses the nation's collections both of English art and of modern art, is dwarfed by this businessman's skyline. But no matter, since it is a fussy late nineteenth-century affair and the modern additions at the back are no masterpiece either. The most interesting thing about the Tate is that it is built on the site of an enormous prison erected (1812) in accordance with the utilitarian principles of Jeremy Bentham. Its octagonal site still emerges, like a palimpsest, in the arrangements of nearby streets and housing. When the prison was pulled down, the London County Council took the opportunity to put up the tree-lined Millbank Estate, the first attempt to provide high-quality working-class flats in a pleasant setting; and Westminster City Council followed this in the later Twenties with Sir Edwin Lutyens' magnificent council flats on Page Street and Vincent Street, whose chequerboard façades and Art Deco entrances show that he could provide grandeur for the poor as well as the rich.

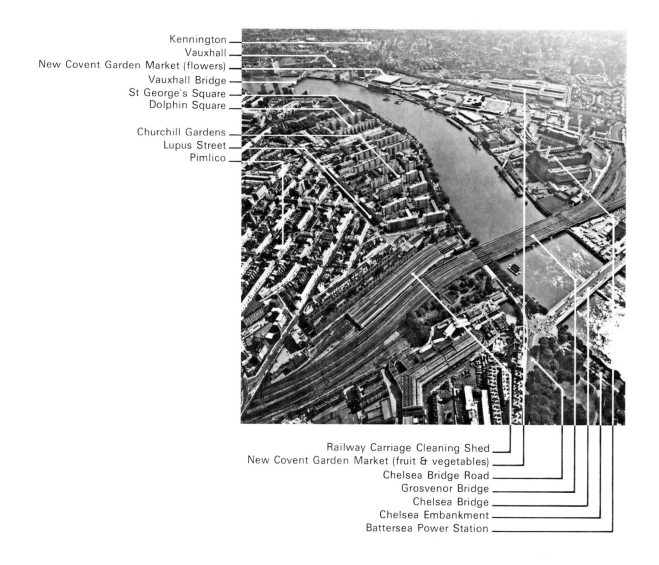

Kennington
Vauxhall
New Covent Garden Market (flowers)
Vauxhall Bridge
St George's Square
Dolphin Square
Churchill Gardens
Lupus Street
Pimlico

Railway Carriage Cleaning Shed
New Covent Garden Market (fruit & vegetables)
Chelsea Bridge Road
Grosvenor Bridge
Chelsea Bridge
Chelsea Embankment
Battersea Power Station

PIMLICO

The district between Vauxhall Bridge and Chelsea Bridge is called after Ben Pimlico, an early seventeenth-century Chelsea publican, who produced fine eponymous nut-brown ale. Until about 1800 it was all market gardens. That function is now served across the river, for the vast district beyond Battersea Power Station and Nine Elms Lane is occupied by the New Covent Garden Market, with the square Flower Market on the left and the twin oblong Fruit and Vegetable Market on the right. The market gardens were swept away between 1825 and 1850, when Cubitt, the great builder, divided a huge chunk of the Grosvenor estates into terraces and squares. In modern Pimlico there are now distinct types of housing which can plainly be seen in the picture. On the left, west of Lupus Street, are Cubitt's early Victorian terraces, now rapidly being upgraded and re-gentrified. At the top, between St George's Square and Claverton Street, is Dolphin Square,

the work of another great builder, Sir Richard Costain. Here in 1937, on the 7.5 acre site of a former Army depot, Costain built Europe's largest block of high-quality flats, 1,236 of them, with attached restaurants, garages, shops, gardens and sports facilities. Below Claverton Street, and by way of social and aesthetic contrast, is the huge estate commissioned by Westminster Council in 1946 and known as Churchill Gardens. It has rather more dwellings (1,661) than Dolphin Square, but grouped in separate blocks of varying heights. The scheme was completed in the 1960s and was much praised by architectural critics, who looked down their noses at Dolphin Square. But as the wheel of taste moves on, Dolphin Square is now more admired, though people actually want to live (of course) in a Cubitt terrace.

PIMLICO REFUSE BARGES

In his book *Rubbish Theory* (Oxford, 1979) Michael Thompson advances the idea that the real difference between the rich and the poor is that a rich man makes use of his rubbish while a poor man simply throws his away. The axiom was illustrated by the millionaire builder Thomas Cubitt, who used the earth he excavated in hollowing out the new St Katharine's Dock to level up sites in Belgravia on which to build his palatial houses. London from Roman times has been built to a great extent on rubbish, but nowadays it generates so much rubbish itself that it has to be carted elsewhere, for all kinds of useful purposes.

So a good deal of furtive transporting take place, of which ordinary Londoners know little. This stylish modernistic building (1967–71) at Cringle Dock just east of Chelsea Bridge is the City of Westminster Refuse Transfer Station. Westminster's rubbish is delivered here by dustcart and is then loaded on barges. It is transported down the Thames, up the creeks to the west of Canvey Island and then dumped on the mysterious Pitsea Marshes near Basildon New Town. There it forms part of a land-reclamation scheme which will produce yet more goods for London to consume and convert into rubbish.

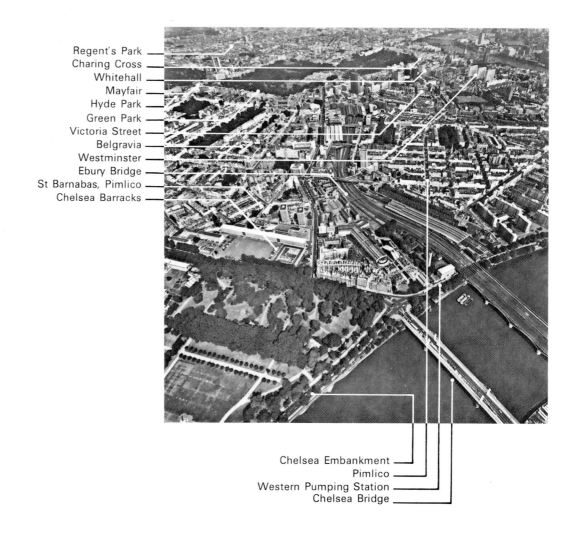

Regent's Park —
Charing Cross —
Whitehall —
Mayfair —
Hyde Park —
Green Park —
Victoria Street —
Belgravia —
Westminster —
Ebury Bridge —
St Barnabas, Pimlico —
Chelsea Barracks —

Chelsea Embankment —
Pimlico —
Western Pumping Station —
Chelsea Bridge —

VICTORIA

Apart from anything else, this vast panorama shows the extent to which the river loops and bends through central London: a straight line drawn north-east from the top of Chelsea Bridge would hit the Thames again at Charing Cross, cutting off all Whitehall and Westminster. Here, Victoria Station and its tracks to Kent and Sussex form the centre of the picture. It was built in the early 1860s, along with a luxury hotel called (inevitably) the Grosvenor. The hotel, by J. T. Knowles, was in the fashionable French Second Empire style, so it was natural for Emile Zola to live there when he fled from arrest in the Dreyfus Case in 1898. To the right of Victoria is Pimlico and beyond it Westminster. To the left is Belgravia. Below Ebury Bridge which carries the Pimlico Road over the railway is the indeterminate area where Pimlico merges into Chelsea. Once it was the site of

Ranelagh Gardens, the biggest north bank amusement park of the eighteenth century. Some of the gardens remain, merging into the park of Chelsea Royal Hospital in the foreground. The rest is now occupied by the 1960s modernism of Chelsea Barracks, with its long, low range of bachelor soldiers' quarters in front, two 15-storey towers for married men behind. Just north of the barracks is another Cundy church, St Barnabas (it is technically possible to spot six Cundy churches in this picture). In the foreground, next to the railway bridge, is the much-admired Western Pumping Station, dating from 1875, which contains some spectacular Victorian machinery. Much prettier, however, is Chelsea Bridge itself, a superbly simplified suspension type which is not, as many suppose, Victorian, but is only half a century old (1934).

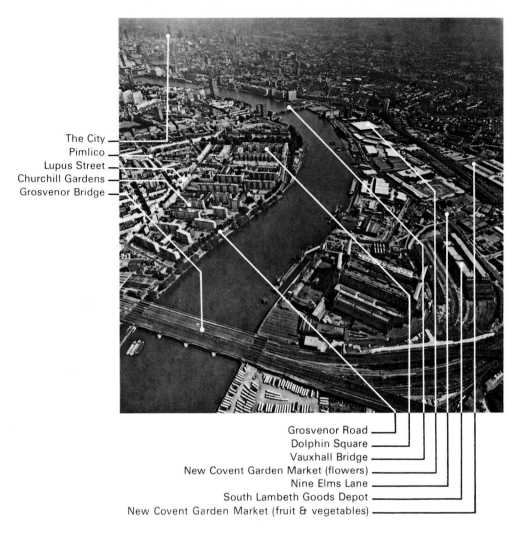

The City —
Pimlico —
Lupus Street —
Churchill Gardens —
Grosvenor Bridge —

Grosvenor Road —
Dolphin Square —
Vauxhall Bridge —
New Covent Garden Market (flowers) —
Nine Elms Lane —
South Lambeth Goods Depot —
New Covent Garden Market (fruit & vegetables) —

BATTERSEA POWER STATION

In the 1920s a determined effort was made to bring the British electricity supply industry up to the standards of the best American models, and the idea of a national grid – the first in the world – was conceived. It was put into operation in the 1930s and involved producing a new generation of power stations, using the existing technology of steam turbines and water-tube boilers but built to a giant size involving huge economies of scale. The more romantic spirits in the industry referred to them as Temples of Power and the best architects were sought to design them and stress the majestic forces they embodied. The most spectacular was the one built at Battersea, 1929–34, for the London Power Company. Section A was designed by Halliday and Agate, with Sir Giles Gilbert Scott, to house a set of 105 megawatt generators, the largest ever seen in Europe. In 1944 Section B, its mirror-image, was commissioned, and the fourth chimney was not raised until 1955. The massive structure with its great fluted chimney stacks – an ironic reference, perhaps, to the four towers of Archer's Smith Square church on the north bank – filled Londoners with awe. Here is industrial architecture at its most sublime, yet despite the superb materials and workmanship the capital cost was only £14,000–£16,000 per megawatt and Battersea electricity was remarkably cheap. Churchill Gardens and Dolphin Square across the river also received free heating from Battersea as a by-product. The station immediately established itself, and has remained one of the best-known landmarks on London's river. But the Central Electricity Generating Board phased it out at the beginning of the 1980s and the question now arises of what to do with this colossal pile of masonry. Pull it down? Preserve it intact? Transform its shell into a museum of industrial art? No answer at the time of writing, and the Temple of Power looks like ending as 'bare, ruined choirs . . .'.

Wandsworth —
Clapham —
Battersea —
Battersea Park —
Albert Bridge —
Cheyne Walk —
Chelsea Embankment —
Chelsea Bridge —
Royal Hospital —
Royal Hospital Road —
Lower Sloane Street —
Chelsea Barracks —
King's Road —
Sloane Square —
Bourne Street —

Sloane Street —
Peter Jones —
Royal Avenue —
Battersea Bridge —
Markham Square —

CHELSEA

Chelsea really begins with Sloane Square (foreground), the King's Road forming the main east–west axis. Of course in Tudor times, when Chelsea was still a village, the thoroughfare was the Thames, Sir Thomas More's house (1520) being built near the river on what is now Beaufort Street, the gardens running inland to the King's Road. Of the old houses of Chelsea few survive, exceptions being Argyle House on the King's Road and Gough House (1707), now part of the Victoria Hospital for Children. More's Chelsea is gone, replaced by the artists' and writers' riverside colony which grew up in the eighteenth and nineteenth centuries: Carlyle lived at 24 Cheyne Row, Rossetti at 16 Cheyne Walk and Turner at number 119. Meanwhile, Charles II, again inspired by Evelyn, had created the Royal Hospital for soldiers, further east along the river (1682–9). It was the Army equivalent of Greenwich Naval Hospital, though imitated from Louis XIV's Invalides. Again, Wren was the principal architect. The Hospital still

flourishes, with 200 red-coated residents, and it is not the only military institution in Chelsea: apart from the barracks, there is the splendid new Army Museum on Tite Street and, just off Sloane Square at the beginning of King's Road, the Duke of York's barracks (1801). The Albert Bridge, an elaborate suspension affair of 1873 and the wrought-iron Battersea Bridge (1890) which replaced the old wooden bridge shown in Whistler's nocturnes, straddle old Chelsea. Beyond, on the right bank, are Fulham and Hammersmith and yet another rail bridge taking British Rail's West London Line south of the river. The south bank here is dominated by Battersea Park, most romantic of the nineteenth-century municipal gardens of London, with a 15-acre boating lake and, since the war, a display of open-air sculpture from Moore to Hepworth. Beyond are Clapham, Wandsworth and, in the far distance, Putney.

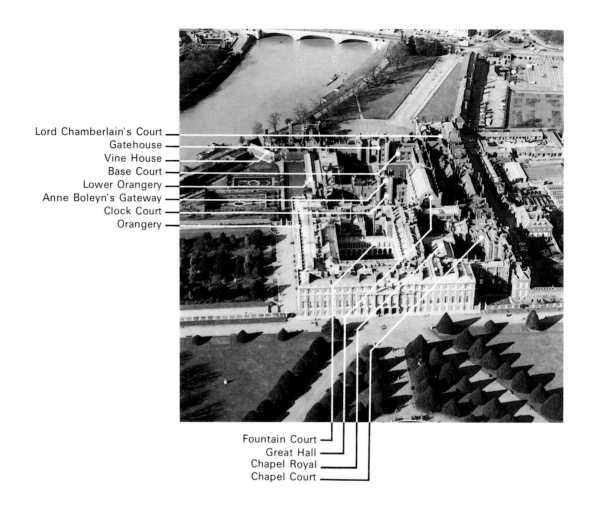

Lord Chamberlain's Court —
Gatehouse —
Vine House —
Base Court —
Lower Orangery —
Anne Boleyn's Gateway —
Clock Court —
Orangery —

Fountain Court —
Great Hall —
Chapel Royal —
Chapel Court —

HAMPTON COURT

Hampton Court Palace is the creation of the greatest pluralist of the late Middle Ages, Thomas Cardinal Wolsey. The son of an Ipswich butcher, he rose through hard work and attention to Henry VIII's whims. He bought Hampton Manor from the Knights of St John in 1514, the year he accumulated two bishoprics as well as the Archbishopric of York, He built the west front and gatehouse, the Base Court and the Clock Court, all in the Tudor Perpendicular style, plus a multitude of other buildings (now gone), making a house of 300 by 600 feet, larger even than the château of Chambord which the French king François I was piling up at the same time. After Henry broke Wolsey in 1529 and took the house, he added the enormous great hall, huge beer and wine cellars, a stupendous kitchen and chapel, a tennis court and tiltyard. Queen Elizabeth nearly died here of smallpox, and James I used it for his Hampton Court Conference (1604) when he tried to make peace between the warring religious factions. From 1689

William and Mary extended the palace as the equivalent of Louis XIV's Versailles, using Wren as architect. He produced the splendid Fountain Court (foreground), and under Queen Anne the orangery, on the south side of the Base Court, which is now used to house Mantegna's cartoons of the Triumph of Caesar. At the same time the elaborate gardens, which included a vinery and a maze, were laid out on the model of Le Nôtre's at Versailles by Henry Wise and George London, with spectacular ironwork gates by Jean Tijou. A contemporary of William wrote that the gardens included 'some snug places of retirement in certain towers, formerly intended as places of accommodation for the king's mistresses'. These have now gone but Hampton Court retains the layout and atmosphere of a baroque palace, together with a strong whiff of Tudor domesticity, for all six of Henry VIII's wives slept here.

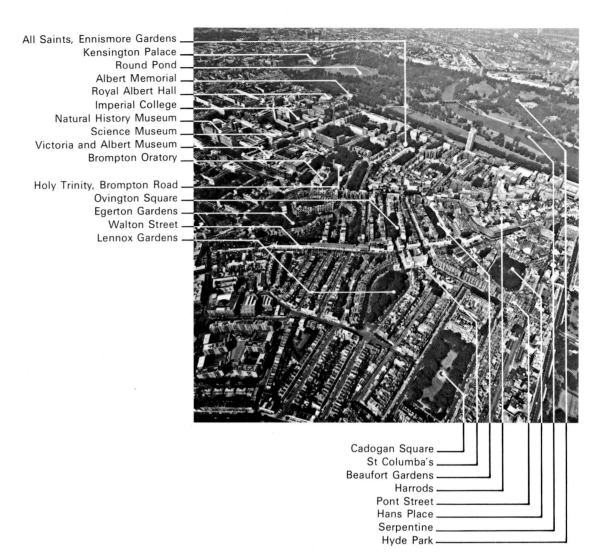

All Saints, Ennismore Gardens
Kensington Palace
Round Pond
Albert Memorial
Royal Albert Hall
Imperial College
Natural History Museum
Science Museum
Victoria and Albert Museum
Brompton Oratory

Holy Trinity, Brompton Road
Ovington Square
Egerton Gardens
Walton Street
Lennox Gardens

Cadogan Square
St Columba's
Beaufort Gardens
Harrods
Pont Street
Hans Place
Serpentine
Hyde Park

BROMPTON

West of Sloane Street and south of Hyde Park lies the quintessential London of the nineteenth-century upper middle class. This part of the metropolis has changed less than you might think, for the overwhelming majority of buildings in this district are still private residences, albeit flats rather than whole houses. The characteristic style is late nineteenth-century brick and terracotta, christened 'Pont Street Dutch'. And there is plenty of greenery in the many private gardens: Hans Place and Cadogan Square on the eastern side; then Lennox Gardens at the western end of Pont Street and, north of Walton Street (from east to west), Beaufort Gardens, Ovington Square, Egerton Terrace, and the elegant curves of Egerton Gardens. In the midst of this, between Basil Street and the Brompton Road, is the immense block of Harrods, also in terracotta, where the locals shop. They pray, if they are Anglican, in Holy Trinity, Brompton Road, if they are Russian Orthodox in Lewis Vulliamy's All Saints, Ennismore Gardens (1846), if they are Catholics in Herbert Gribble's tremendous Italian baroque Brompton Oratory (1878), and

if they are Church of Scotland in the modernistic St Columba's on Walton Street, reputed to be the richest church in London. If they want culture they have only to walk past Brompton Oratory to enter what has been called 'Academic Kensington', created by Prince Albert in the 1850s and continued and completed after his death in 1861. Next to the Oratory is the Victoria and Albert Museum (1860s), in mauve-coloured brick and terracotta, designed in what is termed the Renaissance Lombard Style. The next huge block contains the core of Albertland: the Natural History Museum (1875), behind it the Science Museum (1909) with the Geological Museum adjoining, and behind them both the Imperial College of Science and Technology (1900), with its high tower. Behind them all stands the Royal College of Music (1883), next to Captain Fowke's tremendous domed Albert Hall (1867). Finally, at the Kensington Gore entrance to the park is Albert's own Memorial (1863) by Sir George Gilbert Scott, with beyond it the Round Pond and Kensington Palace.

Hyde Park
Prince's Gardens
Victoria and Albert Museum
Exhibition Road
Science Museum
Natural History Museum

Queen's Gate
Cromwell Road
Geological Museum

NATURAL HISTORY MUSEUM

Opinions vary about the architectural merits of Academic Kensington, though there is no doubt about its general popularity: the Science Museum, for instance, gets more visitors than any other museum in Britain. On the north side of the complex the centrepiece is the Albert Hall, with the Memorial opposite. On the south side all eyes fix on the Natural History Museum, built in the 1870s by the Lancashire architect Alfred Waterhouse. He made his name in the Gothic style and achieved immortal fame in the north with his magnificent Manchester Town Hall, but for this museum he turned to Roman-

esque for inspiration, using its curved arches and stubby towers as motifs, but in a scheme which is totally original. Waterhouse was a brilliant water-colourist, with a delicate feeling for tints, and what makes this building so spectacular (now it has been cleaned) is the contrasts of pale blue and fawn terracotta. Cleaning has also revealed the details of the striking animal and nature sculptures with which Waterhouse adorned the façade, and which reflect the treasures within – not least the half million butterfly specimens and the thousand British wildflowers.

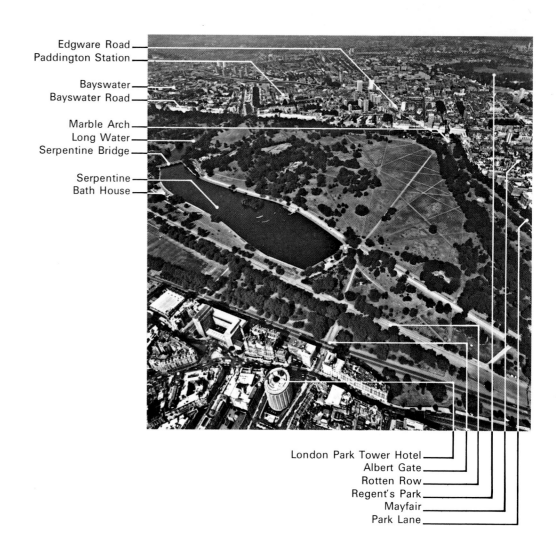

Edgware Road
Paddington Station

Bayswater
Bayswater Road

Marble Arch
Long Water
Serpentine Bridge

Serpentine
Bath House

London Park Tower Hotel
Albert Gate
Rotten Row
Regent's Park
Mayfair
Park Lane

HYDE PARK

Hyde Park was really created by Henry VIII, who knocked together over 600 acres of Abbey land in the 1530s, including the manor of Hyde, and turned it into a deer park. It was sold by the Commonwealth, but the Crown bought it back at the Restoration. William III and George III gradually reduced it to about 400 acres by forming Kensington Gardens. The line of demarcation between the two parks runs along the Long Water, the Serpentine Bridge, and the road which leads to Alexandra Gate. Charles I opened the park to the public but you had to be 'respectably dressed' to get in. The park was the parade-ground of high fashion until the 1830s, especially at the Park Lane end and on Rotten Row (a corruption of *route du roi*). In its heyday just after the Napoleonic Wars people with inferior horses or carriages were kept out. 'Nor did you see', Captain Gronow wrote in his memoirs,

'any of the lower or middle classes of London intruding themselves in regions which, with a sort of tacit understanding, were then given up exclusively to persons of rank and fashion'. There were still cattle and deer in the park in those days. From the 1820s it was beautified, and in the process democratized. The old Westbourne brook was dammed to produce the Serpentine, and George Rennie's pretty bridge thrown across it in 1826. New gates were put up all round, and in 1851 Marble Arch was transported from Buckingham Palace to the old site of Tyburn Gallows, now Speakers' Corner. The Tea House and the Bath House for Serpentine bathers came in 1908, and a restaurant was added as recently as 1963. The prettiest part of the park is the Italian Garden (1861) at Marlborough Gate, but Albert Gate in daffodil time is the most striking.

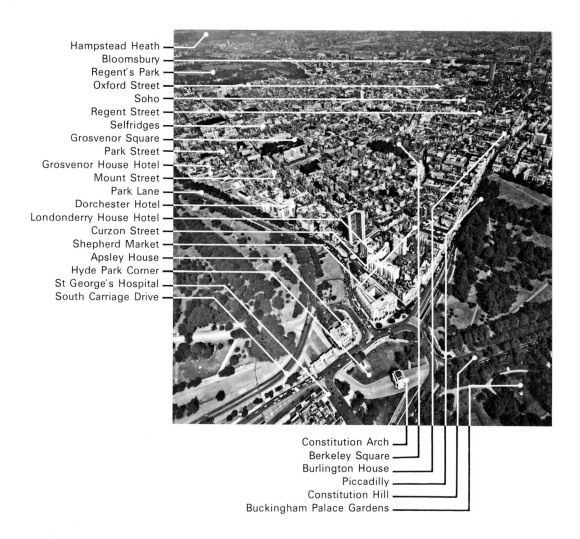

Hampstead Heath —
Bloomsbury —
Regent's Park —
Oxford Street —
Soho —
Regent Street —
Selfridges —
Grosvenor Square —
Park Street —
Grosvenor House Hotel —
Mount Street —
Park Lane —
Dorchester Hotel —
Londonderry House Hotel —
Curzon Street —
Shepherd Market —
Apsley House —
Hyde Park Corner —
St George's Hospital —
South Carriage Drive —

Constitution Arch —
Berkeley Square —
Burlington House —
Piccadilly —
Constitution Hill —
Buckingham Palace Gardens —

MAYFAIR

Mayfair, bounded by Oxford Street, Regent Street, Park Lane and Piccadilly, gets its name from the cattle fair held from 1686 at the Hyde Park Corner end of Piccadilly, in an open space called Brookfield. The 'brook' was the Tyburn, which originated south of Hampstead. Its route across Mayfair can still be traced along South Molton Lane, Avery Row, Lansdowne Passage and White Horse Street, where Shepherd Market, laid out by Edward Shepherd in 1735, runs into Piccadilly. The Berkeleys, the main landlords in the south-east, began to lay out Berkeley Square and the neighbouring streets (Bruton, Farm, Hill and Charles) in the 1670s. From the 1720s, Sir Richard Grosvenor, whose father had married Mary Davies, heiress to north-west Mayfair, developed the six-acre Grosvenor Square and the streets between Mount Street and Oxford Street. In the eighteenth and nineteenth centuries most of the great politicos lived in Mayfair, mainly overlooking Park Lane or Piccadilly. Disraeli's house was at the corner of Upper Grosvenor Street. Palmerston's was on Piccadilly and is now the Naval and Military Club. None of the old houses is now privately owned. On Park Lane, Brook House, Dudley House and Stanhope House are offices; Grosvenor House and Dorchester House have been replaced by hotels. So has Londonderry House, which as recently as the 1950s still belonged to the family. Crewe House, on Curzon Street, stands yet, but is a company headquarters. Devonshire House on Piccadilly is a car saleroom. Lansdowne House survives in part as a club. Burlington House is the Royal Academy. The best reminder of old Mayfair is Albany off Piccadilly. Originally Melbourne House, it was converted into bachelor apartments by Henry Holland in 1803, and has since housed many notable ones from Macaulay to Edward Heath. Another survivor is the Albemarle Street premises of the publishers John Murray, virtually untouched since the time when Byron held court in them. But the best address in Britain is still Wellington's old home, Apsley House: Number One, London.

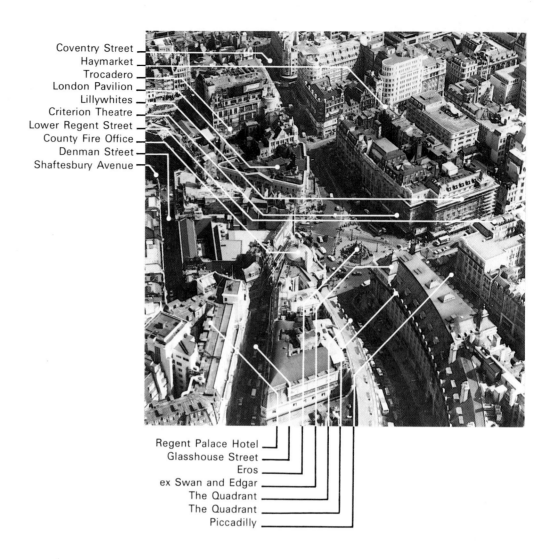

Coventry Street
Haymarket
Trocadero
London Pavilion
Lillywhites
Criterion Theatre
Lower Regent Street
County Fire Office
Denman Street
Shaftesbury Avenue

Regent Palace Hotel
Glasshouse Street
Eros
ex Swan and Edgar
The Quadrant
The Quadrant
Piccadilly

PICCADILLY CIRCUS

Town planners have found London a frustrating place. The Prince Regent's favourite architect, John Nash, planned a triumphant route from Carlton House up Lower Regent Street, along Regent Street, up Portland Place and so into Regent's Park. Piccadilly Circus and Oxford Circus were to be grandiose pauses on this progress. But the scheme was never completed and little now remains of any of it. From 1905 on, old Regent Street was pulled down bit by bit and replaced. The present buildings around the Circus are undistinguished and uncoordinated: the London Pavilion (1885), the Quadrant (1910), the County Fire Office (1924) and the Criterion Theatre (1870). The Eros fountain in the middle, designed by Alfred Gilbert in the 1890s, makes no sense at all. For it is supposed to commemorate the austere

philanthropist and dour Low Church fundamentalist Lord Shaftesbury, who believed in the imminence of the Second Coming and other Bible-thumping notions. What was Eros to him? The choice of Eros, however, does suit the usage ordinary people have made of the Circus. More suburbanites and provincials have arranged to meet outside what was once Swan and Edgar's (1917) than any other address in the capital and the Circus is the normal gathering-point for hell-raisers. It is vulgar, garish, rather dirty, ugly, commercial, tremendously unartistic and immoral; and most people love it. Attempts to rebuild it all according to the aesthetic dictates of modern architecture have thus run into insuperable difficulties, and the Circus awaits another, and jollier, age for its transformation.

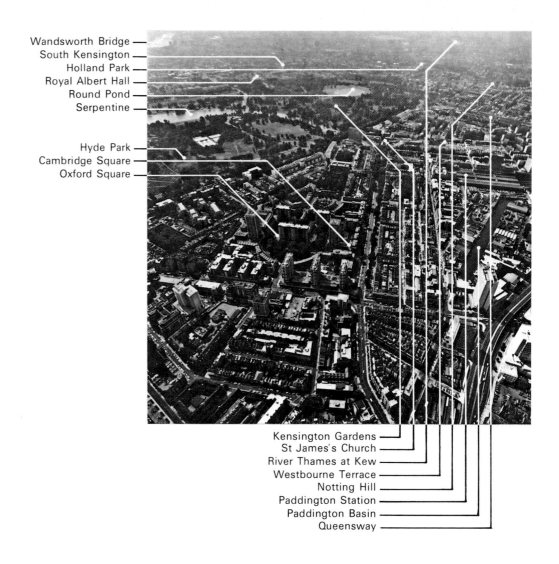

Wandsworth Bridge —
South Kensington —
Holland Park —
Royal Albert Hall —
Round Pond —
Serpentine —

Hyde Park —
Cambridge Square —
Oxford Square —

Kensington Gardens —
St James's Church —
River Thames at Kew —
Westbourne Terrace —
Notting Hill —
Paddington Station —
Paddington Basin —
Queensway —

BAYSWATER

In Victorian times Bayswater, which runs from the Edgware Road to Notting Hill Gate, was regarded as 'the wrong side of the Park'. Members of Galsworthy's Forsyte clan lived there until they had made their pile; then crossed over. It is still dead-centre middle class, though coming up in the world. Here we can see how it fits into the jigsaw of west London. Hyde Park and the Serpentine are on the left, with Kensington Gardens and the Round Pond in the centre. Beyond lies South Kensington, merging into Holland Park, and then Notting Hill on the right. Further still in the distance the Thames appears twice: on the left, at Wandsworth Bridge, and again on the right at Kew. In the eighteenth century there was nothing in Bayswater except market gardens and odd isolated houses, like Mrs Siddons's in Westbourne Grove. Then in 1795 William Praed built a canal from Uxbridge to the Paddington Basin, and this was pushed around Nash's new Regent's Park to link up with the lower Thames at Regent's Canal

Dock. Thus Praed Street came into existence, and in the mid-1830s it was chosen as the Paddington terminus for the new Great Western Railway. Meanwhile, Tyburn Gallows had been abolished in 1827, and the Bishopric of London developed its land west of it as a series of squares and crescents along the axis of Sussex Gardens. The idea was to call the area Tyburnia, on the model of Belgravia, but not surprisingly the name did not catch on. At the end of Sussex Gardens stood the new parish church of St James, enlarged in the 1880s by G.E. Street, and one of the most impressive Gothic Revival churches in London. The series of crescents around Oxford and Cambridge Squares have been developed as high-rise luxury flats, but many hundreds of the old stucco terraces are left and (now that they are being modernized) provide some of the best and prettiest housing in London.

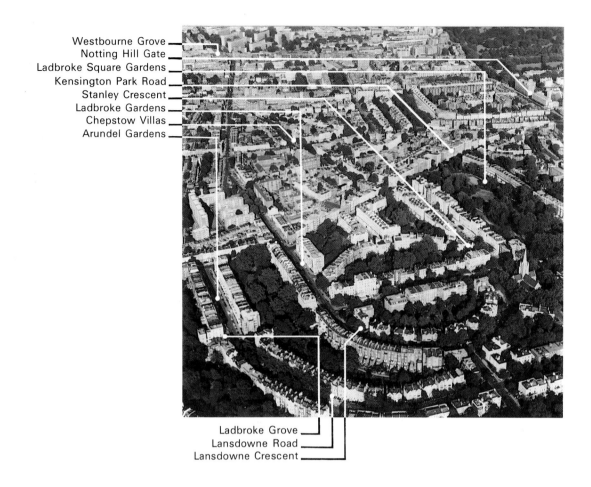

Westbourne Grove
Notting Hill Gate
Ladbroke Square Gardens
Kensington Park Road
Stanley Crescent
Ladbroke Gardens
Chepstow Villas
Arundel Gardens

Ladbroke Grove
Lansdowne Road
Lansdowne Crescent

NOTTING HILL

As recently as the 1830s this part of London was still open space. Only two hundred yards away, that is across the present Holland Park Road, was Holland Park itself, home of the Fox family, the last big country house to be swallowed up by the spread of the metropolis. At Notting Hill there was a race course called the Hippodrome. Then, in about 1840, the owners of the Ladbroke Estate drove a beautiful wide road, Ladbroke Grove, through the middle of the race course and, following the outline of its tracks, laid out a series of crescents on either side of the Ladbroke Grove axis. The picture shows Stanley Crescent, Ladbroke Gardens and Ladbroke Square Gardens above the axis, and Lans-

downe Crescent, Lansdowne Road, Elgin Crescent and Blenheim Crescent below it, arranged concentrically. The houses are spacious, though by no means grand, and the great feature of the development is the generous space allotted for tree-filled communal gardens. Here is early Victorian London at its best. Victorian housing used to be seen as an abyss of unimaginative bad taste between Regency elegance and late nineteenth-century Garden City utopianism. In fact the Ladbroke Estate, which is largely untouched by twentieth-century development, shows that early Victorian planners were skilled at realizing the vision of *rus in urbe*.

Empire Way
Wembley Hill Road
Conference Centre
Arena (ex Empire Swimming Pool)
South Way
Stadium

WEMBLEY

Which is older, football or Wembley? Probably Wembley, since it occurs in a charter of 825 and means Wemba's farm. English football is old too, to judge by the number of times it was condemned by medieval monarchs as illegal because it was conducive to violence and hooliganism. But it survived and by Shakespeare's day (*Comedy of Errors*, Act II) the balls were already made of leather. After the Restoration the government gave up trying to ban it, and by 1863 a Football Association had been formed to codify the rules. The first International (England *v.* Scotland) came a decade later, and by the end of the 1880s we were exporting it to Europe as well as the Empire. The Empire Stadium, with its four domed towers and concrete façades, was designed in the early Twenties by J.M. Simpson of the firm of Simpson & Ayrton. In 1923 the first Football Association Cup Final was played here, Bolton beating West Ham 2–nil. The next year

it was the centrepiece of the British Empire Exhibition, being used for the International Rodeo and the Searchlight Tattoo. The Exhibition's aim was to drum up trade within the Empire, but when it closed in 1925 most of the pavilions were demolished or allowed to decay. The Empire Pool (now Wembley Arena) was built to Olympic standards in 1934 and both stadium and pool were used for the fourteenth Olympic Games in 1948. Wembley Stadium and its surrounds have an ineffacable inter-war flavour: the push of the Metropolitan Railway and the Bakerloo line into the outer, tree-lined suburbs, Wembley Park housing and the cult of Metroland (even the tube trains had 'Live in Metroland' engraved on the carriage handles) all symbolized Twenties optimism. The stadium is now gloriously period too; it conjures up, as Simon Jenkins puts it, 'a world of Brylcreem, shin pads and goalies in flat caps'.

HARROW SCHOOL

Eton College and Harrow School have inspired extraordinary affection from their alumni, yet they are utterly different. Eton is low-lying, riverine, medieval; Harrow is airy, on the Hill – from which thirteen counties can be glimpsed – and it is visually very Victorian. It does indeed go back to 1572 when John Lyon 'provided a free grammar schoole in this parish to have continuance for ever'. But rich folks sent their boys there because it was healthier than Eton, Winchester or Westminster, and by the mid-eighteenth century it was one of the 'Great Schools'. It straggles all over the Hill, merging with the town, and is pretty formless, though for the past two centuries it has always employed the best architects. C.R. Cockerell designed the Old School, Sir George Gilbert Scott the Chapel and Library, William Burges the Speech Room and Sir Herbert Baker the War Memorial Building. Harrow has produced seven prime ministers, four of them outstanding: Palmerston, Sir Robert Peel, Stanley Baldwin and Winston Churchill. They loved the place. Palmerston kept some of his old Harrow exam papers until the end of his life, Baldwin confided that he hoped 'to form a cabinet worthy of Harrow', and Churchill attended its famous annual sing-song until he was nearly ninety, weeping copiously on each occasion. Even Byron, who hated virtually everything else English, loved his old school, constantly recalling the days when he sloped off to the parish churchyard, to write poetry lying on the flat tomb of one John Peachey.

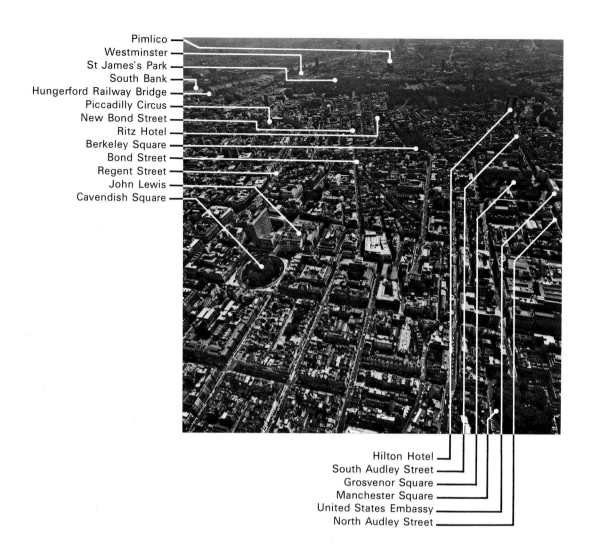

Pimlico —
Westminster —
St James's Park —
South Bank —
Hungerford Railway Bridge —
Piccadilly Circus —
New Bond Street —
Ritz Hotel —
Berkeley Square —
Bond Street —
Regent Street —
John Lewis —
Cavendish Square —

Hilton Hotel —
South Audley Street —
Grosvenor Square —
Manchester Square —
United States Embassy —
North Audley Street —

SHOPPERS' LONDON

This picture covers such a large and important span of London that we had better proceed systematically. In the far distance is the south bank. The curve of the Thames moves from the Hungerford Railway Bridge at Charing Cross on the left, to Battersea Park on the right. Then come Westminster, Pimlico and Chelsea. The belt of trees and grass is St James's Park and Green Park, with Buckingham Palace in the middle. The skyscraper in the top right-hand corner is the Hilton Hotel on Park Lane, and from it runs the straight line of South and North Audley Street, hitting Oxford Street at right angles at the corner of Selfridges. Off Audley Street are Grosvenor Square (left) and the US Embassy (right). Beyond, near the centre of the picture, are the trees of Berkeley Square. Bond Street and New Bond Street run from the Piccadilly side of Green Park down to the middle of the picture, bisecting Oxford Street. Then Oxford Street continues to the left (that

is, east) to Oxford Circus, from which Regent Street pushes south until it curves round to meet Piccadilly Circus. You might call this Shoppers' London. It is also luxury London, for it includes virtually the whole of Mayfair, seen this time from the north. At the point where Berkeley Street joins Piccadilly stands the Ritz. Claridges can be seen at the corner of Davies Street and Brook Street. The Connaught Hotel is two blocks below Grosvenor Square, opposite the Mount Street HQ of the Jesuits. In the foreground is the beginning of Marylebone, and Marylebone Lane runs crookedly through the later neat blocks laid out by the developers of estates owned by the Dukes of Portland and Newcastle, as is reflected in virtually all the street names. The circular bit of greenery is Cavendish Square, with Manchester Square in the bottom right-hand corner.

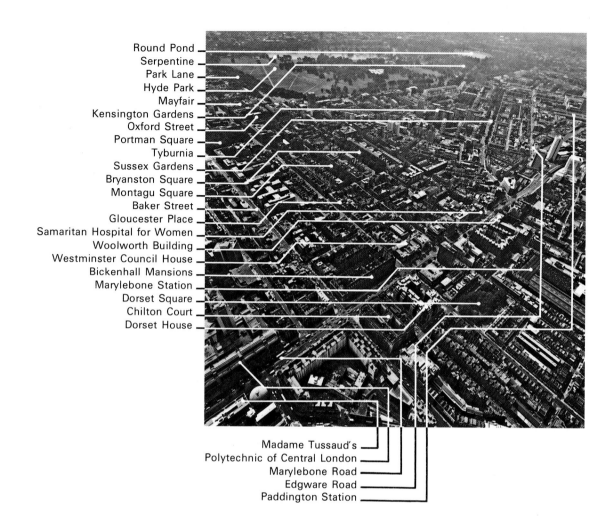

Round Pond
Serpentine
Park Lane
Hyde Park
Mayfair
Kensington Gardens
Oxford Street
Portman Square
Tyburnia
Sussex Gardens
Bryanston Square
Montagu Square
Baker Street
Gloucester Place
Samaritan Hospital for Women
Woolworth Building
Westminster Council House
Bickenhall Mansions
Marylebone Station
Dorset Square
Chilton Court
Dorset House

Madame Tussaud's
Polytechnic of Central London
Marylebone Road
Edgware Road
Paddington Station

SHERLOCK HOLMES'S LONDON

The name Marylebone comes from Mary-le-Bourne, or brook, the same Tyburn brook that runs through Mayfair. At the beginning of the eighteenth century it was a village surrounded by open space and parkland, some of which is still incorporated in Regent's Park. In the eighteenth century it became part of the West End, and in the nineteenth it encompassed what might be called Sherlock Holmes's London. Baker Street, running diagonally across the foreground of the picture, was laid out in the 1790s and rapidly became one of the great arteries of the capital. Holmes called London 'that great cesspool into which all the loungers of the Empire are irresistibly drained'. Certainly, Holmes's lodgings, near where Baker Street intersects the Marylebone Road, were a good point of vantage. To the left is Madame Tussaud's (1884), opposite the Polytechnic of Central London (1960s). While Holmes was chasing the Hound of the Baskervilles,

Bickenhall Mansions, one of London's first big blocks of purpose-built flats (1896) was going up at the corner of Baker Street and the Marylebone Road. Next to it is Westminster Council House (1914) and Library (1939), both designed by Sir Edwin Cooper. At the centre right of the picture Marylebone Station faces the old Great Central Hotel, long the headquarters of British Rail. In the foreground are two huge blocks of inter-war flats: Chiltern Court (1925) and, on the far side of Baker Street, Dorset House (1935). To the right of the picture Marylebone Road rushes past the Samaritan Hospital for Women (left) and the new Woolworth Building (right) and over the Edgware Road to become Westway. Beyond (left to right) are Paddington, 'Tyburnia' and of course Hyde Park, 'the one fixed point', to quote Holmes on Watson, 'in a changing world'.

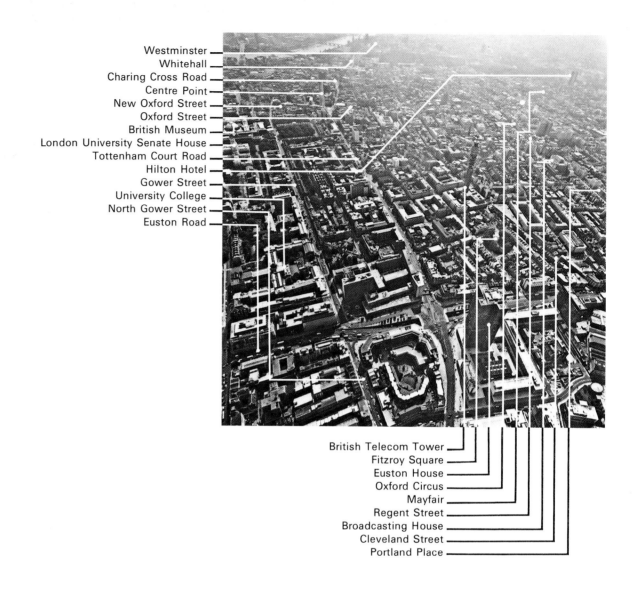

Westminster ——
Whitehall ——
Charing Cross Road ——
Centre Point ——
New Oxford Street ——
Oxford Street ——
British Museum ——
London University Senate House ——
Tottenham Court Road ——
Hilton Hotel ——
Gower Street ——
University College ——
North Gower Street ——
Euston Road ——

British Telecom Tower ——
Fitzroy Square ——
Euston House ——
Oxford Circus ——
Mayfair ——
Regent Street ——
Broadcasting House ——
Cleveland Street ——
Portland Place ——

TOTTENHAM COURT ROAD

This picture also needs a bit of sorting out. The main road in the foreground is the Hampstead Road, descending due south from Camden Town. When it crosses Euston Road (running from right to left in the photo) it becomes Tottenham Court Road, one of the main thoroughfares of west-central London. This is a very ancient road, continuing, after it crosses New Oxford Street and passes the Centre Point skyscraper, in the form of the Charing Cross Road. Having crossed Trafalgar Square it then leads, as Whitehall, straight to Westminster. Running parallel to Tottenham Court Road on the left is Gower Street, which effectively divides Marylebone from Bloomsbury. Hence, below Euston Road and left of Gower Street we have, in order, University College, the central buildings of London

University, and then the British Museum, with Holborn beyond. In the foreground of the picture, opposite Warren Street tube station, is the big skyscraper of Euston House, and beneath it the headquarters of Capital Radio and Thames TV. Four blocks down from the Euston Road, on the corner of Cleveland Street and Howland Street, is the Post Office Tower (now British Telecom Tower). Beyond it, running diagonally across the top right-hand of the picture, is the broad canyon of Portland Place, curving round Broadcasting House (seen from the rear) where it becomes Regent Street, then crossing Oxford Circus and plunging south to Piccadilly. In the top right-hand corner, across the lush acres of Mayfair, the tower of the Hilton Hotel is a landmark for orientation.

St George's Hotel
Regent Street
Great Portland Street
All Souls, Langham Place
Broadcasting House
Langham Hotel
Portland Place

BROADCASTERS' LONDON

Langham Place and Portland Place illustrate the way in which the British approach the problems of metropolitan planning. One might say the way to muddle is paved with good architectural intentions. Portland Place, which links the great semicircle of Park Crescent to Regent Street, was designed by Robert and James Adam in the mid-1770s. It was then the widest street in London and its houses, though not palaces, very substantial. Nash, in his great scheme to link The Mall to Regent's Park, could not turn Regent Street and Portland Place into a straight line, but he masked the shift from one into the other by slipping in All Souls, Langham Place, one of the most elegant and original churches in the city. The scheme has been completely ruined, since all of Regent Street and most of Portland Place have been rebuilt in haphazard patches. The eighteenth-century house at the bottom of Portland Place was demolished in the 1860s to make way for the old Langham Hotel, described by Pevsner as 'a High Victorian Monster' (at all events incompatible with either Nash or Adam). To crown it all, the burgeoning BBC put up at the beginning of the 1930s its almost shapeless Broadcasting House. This building has become so familiar that most people have even got to like it. But it soon became too small for the ever-expanding Corporation, and did not lend itself to rational extension. The result is that the BBC bureaucracy has expanded all over the surrounding neighbourhood, including the old Langham, adding bits and pieces when necessary. Our photograph illustrates the dog's breakfast thus produced, though to be sure it does not look quite so bad from the ground. The architectural shortcomings of the BBC give added irony to the Latin inscription in the great hall of Broadcasting House, dedicating 'this temple of the arts to Almighty God'.

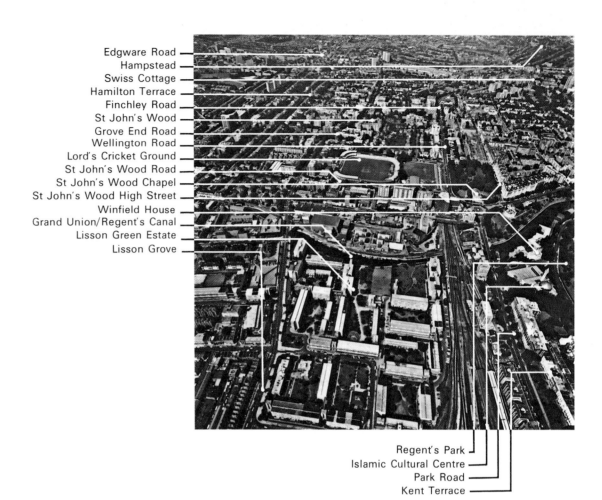

Edgware Road
Hampstead
Swiss Cottage
Hamilton Terrace
Finchley Road
St John's Wood
Grove End Road
Wellington Road
Lord's Cricket Ground
St John's Wood Road
St John's Wood Chapel
St John's Wood High Street
Winfield House
Grand Union/Regent's Canal
Lisson Green Estate
Lisson Grove

Regent's Park
Islamic Cultural Centre
Park Road
Kent Terrace

ST JOHN'S WOOD

This picture faces north-west and to get the orientation right it is necessary to know that the snaky line running from left to right is the Regent's Canal, going from Paddington Basin around the north side of Regent's Park, seen at the right edge of the photo. Marylebone Station is just out of sight at the bottom, and alongside its railway lines runs Park Road, with the Islamic Cultural Centre on its right, then Winfield House, residence of the U S Ambassador. At the circus in front of the pretty Grecian St John's Chapel (1813) by Thomas Hardwick, the road side-steps to the left, past Lord's Cricket Ground, and becomes first Wellington Road then, veering right, the Finchley Road on its way into Hampstead. Beyond Lord's are two parallel roads, Grove End Road and the Edgware Road, pushing on to Maida Vale and Kilburn. The centre of the picture is St John's Wood, which actually was a wood in the sixteenth century, for Babington, the conspirator

who tried to murder Queen Elizabeth, was caught hiding there in 1586. It was developed in the second quarter of the nineteenth century into a region of detached or semi-detached stucco villas, quiet, discreet and umbrageous. Some were occupied by the kept ladies of the rich and aristocratic, but in others the paladins of secular high-mindedness held court: George Eliot, Herbert Spencer, Thomas Huxley and Charles Bradlaugh, as well as artists like Landseer. Many villas and studios were replaced by Thirties blocks of flats, and there have been innumerable post-war developments, such as the enormous Lisson Green Estate in the foreground. But in the quiet streets to the right of Wellington Road many of the original villas survive – though not, alas, the flavour, since they have been largely taken over by diplomats and other expense-account types.

St John's Wood ──
Circus Road ──
Wellington Hospital ──
Grove End Road ──
Wellington Road ──
St John's Wood High Street ──
St John's Wood Road ──
St John's Wood Chapel ──
US Ambassador's Residence ──
Regent's Canal ──
railway line to Marylebone ──

LORD'S CRICKET GROUND

Thomas Lord's ground has been the headquarters of cricket, or to be precise of the Marylebone Cricket Club, since 1814. In those days the game was almost as corrupt and violent as prize-fighting. In the eighteenth century it was criticized by both Church and state for causing labouring men to stay off work, bringing together in an unseemly manner 'gentlemen, clergy and lawyers with butchers and cobblers' and, not least, encouraging gambling. The laws of cricket, established in 1774, made matters worse in the last respect, since regularity encourages scientific betting (and bribery). Under the Regency, it was said, 'Just in front of the Pavilion at Lord's, sat men ready, with money down, to give and take the current odds upon the play'. Cricket violence came to a head in 1817 when Lord's played Nottingham and the magistrates insisted stumps be drawn promptly at seven to avoid a full-scale riot. Thereafter cricket became more sedate, and from late Victorian times until the 1950s gentlemanly behaviour on the pitch, and absolute decorum (including silence during play) among spectators was insisted on. Meanwhile the buildings of Lord's were added to bit by bit, forming what Pevsner dismissed as 'a jumble without aesthetic aspirations, quite unthinkable in a country like Sweden or Holland'. Maybe, but Lord's is much loved, not least because its bars, including the famous Tavern, stay open throughout play. But the old decorum and silence have long gone; bad temper on the pitch, shouting, booing and endless noise off it, threaten to bring Lord's back full cycle to its rumbustious origins.

114

HAMPSTEAD HEATH

Parliament Hill on Hampstead Heath rises to nearly 320 feet, and the Heath has always commanded a fine view over the metropolis to the south. In the seventeenth century Hampstead was nothing but a village, with its heath for common pasture. Then, early in the eighteenth century, it became a resort for Londoners. Belsize Park nearby was a pleasure garden, like Ranelagh or Vauxhall. Hampstead developed its mineral springs (hence, in the village, Well Walk and nearby Flask Walk, where visitors filled their bottles). A few big houses went up in the course of the eighteenth century, and many gentlemen's cottages. Hampstead became a rural resort for people with business in the City, and increasingly a place favoured by writers, intellectuals and members of the well-to-do middle class who liked to be 'different'. In 1880 it had about 5,000 people, and though it grew steadily over the next 150 years, passing the 100,000-mark in the 1950s, it has never lost its sense of independence from the sprawling mass of London or, indeed, its village character. This is thanks to the heath, jealously preserved from development and, next to Wimbledon Common, the wildest bit of country in London. Hampstead's most famous inhabitant was John Keats, who lived in Well Walk, with his friend and fellow poet Leigh Hunt in the nearby Vale of Health. But writers who have worked in Hampstead are legion: Aldous Huxley lived in Bracknell Gardens, from which he studied the habits of Middleton Murry (pilloried in *Point Counter Point*) and his mistress Katherine Mansfield. John Galsworthy reigned, Forsyte-like, in solid Grove Lodge, John Masefield was in Well Walk, D.H. Lawrence in Byron Villas and George Orwell in Mortimer Crescent. Even Dr Johnson lived around the Heath, at Frognal, but found it too rural.

Camden Town
Outer Circle
Aviary
The Zoo
Elephant House
Gloucester Gate
St Katharine's Chapel
Grove House
Bird Sanctuary
Cumberland Terrace
Inner Circle
The Holme
Bedford College
Sussex Place

REGENT'S PARK

Next to Wren, John Nash is probably London's greatest architect. His masterpiece was Regent's Park and its surrounding terraces. Unlike most of his other set-pieces, this survives in its essence, though by no means intact. The idea was *rus in urbe*: that is, a hundred or so large town houses arranged in terraces, plus a few individual villas, all enjoying the rustic amenity of a great ornamental park. The scheme was realized after the Duke of Portland's Crown lease on Marylebone Park ended in 1809. Nash then laid out Regent's Park, at 400-or-so acres a little larger than Hyde Park. He provided it with a 22-acre lake fed by the new Regent's Canal link which he ran round the northern edge. There were two circles, an inner one of ornamental gardens and villas, and an outer of parkland along which he and his successors built stupendous classical terraces fronting on the greenery. There are endless subtle variations in the designs. Indeed in Sussex Place (left foreground) Nash crowned his classical orders with octagonal oriental domes. Across the other side of the park the long panorama of Cumberland Terrace and Gloucester Gate, which form with the park the finest landscape in Europe, is punctuated by Ambrose Poynter's St Katharine's Chapel, modelled on King's College Chapel, Cambridge. Of the Inner Circle villas, one has been swallowed up by London University's Bedford College, but The Holme and Grove House, both by Decimus Burton, remain in more or less their original form. Nearby is the famous Open Air Theatre. Decimus Burton's Zoo occupies the top left-hand corner of the park. Beyond it lies the green space of Primrose Hill, and beyond that Belsize Park and Haverstock Hill. Behind Cumberland Terrace is Camden Town.

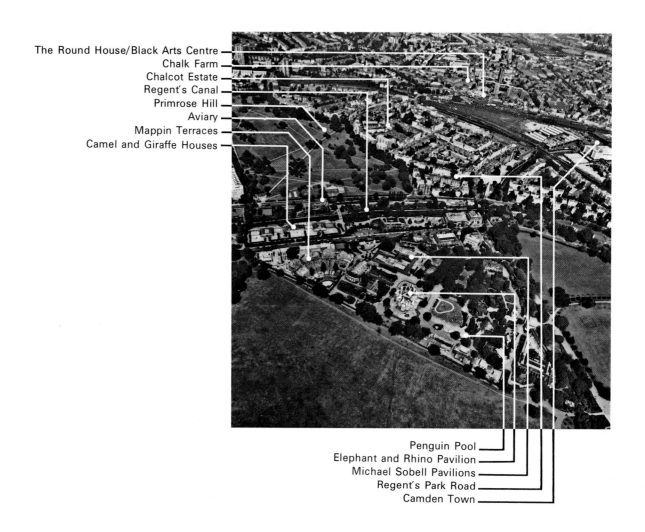

The Round House/Black Arts Centre
Chalk Farm
Chalcot Estate
Regent's Canal
Primrose Hill
Aviary
Mappin Terraces
Camel and Giraffe Houses

Penguin Pool
Elephant and Rhino Pavilion
Michael Sobell Pavilions
Regent's Park Road
Camden Town

REGENT'S PARK ZOO

The Zoological Society Gardens have always been associated with scientific brilliance and architectural innovation. The Society was founded in 1826 by two great men, Sir Stamford Raffles, creator of Singapore, and the chemist Sir Humphry Davy. They commissioned Decimus Burton to lay out the Zoo on both sides of Nash's Outer Circle, under which Burton drove the West Tunnel. Not many of his original buildings have survived, except the 1830s Camel and Giraffe Houses beyond the Circle, since the Zoo authorities have constantly tried to devise new settings which both give the creatures something approaching a natural habitat and increase their visibility to the public. The object has always been to get away from old-fashioned cages. Hence in 1913 the Zoo put up the famous Mappin Terraces for polar bears and penguins, imitated all over the world as the proper way to present animals. During the 1930s, Dr Julian Huxley commissioned a number of highly original settings, including Lubetkin's penguin pool. From the late 1950s onwards the Zoo embarked on an expensive and radical building programme, financed by such tycoons as Jack Cotton and Charles Clore. Some of the results have proved very popular, especially the enormous Elephant and Rhino Pavilion (1965) and the Michael Sobell Pavilions (1972) for gorillas, orang-utangs and other apes. More controversial is the modernistic aviary, designed by Lord Snowdon with the help of Cedric Price and Frank Newby, though its canal-side setting is unquestionably delightful. In the top right-hand corner are the restaurants and beyond them, across the road, are the Society's headquarters, with its fine library of over 100,000 books.

City
Tower Bridge
King's Cross Station
St Pancras Station
St Pancras Church
Friends' House
Euston Station
Wellcome Building
Tottenham Court Road
Euston Tower
Park Square East
Royal College of Physicians
The Broad Walk

Holy Trinity Church
Park Square Gardens
Centre Point
Great Portland Street
Park Square West
Park Crescent
Marylebone Road

EUSTON

Apart from Regent's Park and its terraces, and Carlton House Terrace itself, Park Crescent is the best remaining example of John Nash's vision of how the West End of London should look. Originally he planned it as an enormous circle, then changed the northern half into a garden square, enclosed on its sides by the straight terraces of Park Streets East and West. The Broad Walk cuts right across the east side of Regent's Park to Prince Albert Road on the north of it, and in theory should provide a two-mile perspective down to the bottom of Portland Place. But it is interrupted by the trees of Park Square Gardens and, not least, by Marylebone Road. This is one of London's busiest west–east arteries, linking not only Westway to the East End, but also five of London's principal railway stations. Paddington and Marylebone are out of the picture to the west, but Euston can be seen top left, with its huge expanse of flat roof and the squat glass towers of British Rail

headquarters. Beyond it are St Pancras and King's Cross. The Euston Road-Marylebone Road axis is linked by two of London's finest churches: St Pancras, Woburn Place, opposite Euston, the first (1819) Greek Revival church in the capital, designed by William and Henry Inwood, and beyond the eastern horn of Park Crescent, Holy Trinity (1828) by Sir John Soane, a brilliant exercise in the Ionic. Behind it is the arresting shape of Denys Lasdun's 1962 Royal College of Physicians. Along the Euston Road, just past the skyscraper of the Euston Centre but on the other side, are the Wellcome Museum, the world's largest collection of medical lore, and Friends' House, headquarters of the Quakers. Beyond, to the right, is Islington, backed by the towers of the City of London, with Tower Bridge silhouetted on the horizon.

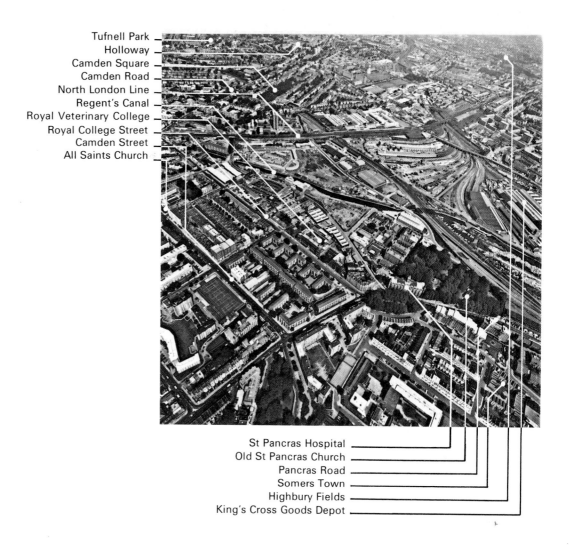

Tufnell Park —
Holloway —
Camden Square —
Camden Road —
North London Line —
Regent's Canal —
Royal Veterinary College —
Royal College Street —
Camden Street —
All Saints Church —

St Pancras Hospital —————
Old St Pancras Church ————
Pancras Road ————
Somers Town ————
Highbury Fields ————
King's Cross Goods Depot ————

CAMDEN TOWN

This picture gives some idea of the devastation inflicted on working-class north London by the railway age. The construction of the old Regent's Canal, which makes its way across this stretch from Camden Town on the left to Pentonville on the right, was nothing by comparison. In Victorian times an enormous area of humble terraced housing was torn down to provide access to the new stations of Euston, St Pancras and King's Cross, and the vast marshalling yards of the King's Cross Goods Depot, seen on the middle right. Dickens knew the area intimately, for his father had moved the family to Somers Town (bottom right-hand corner) shortly after his release from the Marshalsea Prison. Among his best-known characters, Bob Cratchit of *A Christmas Carol* and Traddles and Micawber of *David Copperfield* all lived in Camden Town. In *Dombey and Son* the coming of the railways becomes one of the sinister themes of the book, for the innocent Toodle family lives in Staggs's Gardens, Camden Town:

'The first shock of a great earthquake had, just at that period, rent the whole neighbourhood to its centre. ... Houses were knocked down; streets broken through and stopped; deep pits and trenches dug in the ground; enormous heaps of earth and clay thrown up'. A few years later, 'There was no such place as Staggs's Gardens. It had vanished from the earth'. The scars of this great catastrophe are visible still, though many early nineteenth-century terraces remain, to be sought after and gentrified; they contrast favourably with such vast modern housing estates as Agar Grove, just beyond the Camden Road-Caledonian Road railway, or the Clock Tower estate on North Road behind it. In the centre of the picture, off Royal College Street, is the Royal Veterinary College, with the handsome St Pancras Hospital and Old St Pancras Church to its right providing a little greenery. Centre right, on Camden Street, is another fine Inwood church, All Saints (1822), in the Ionic Greek Revival mode.

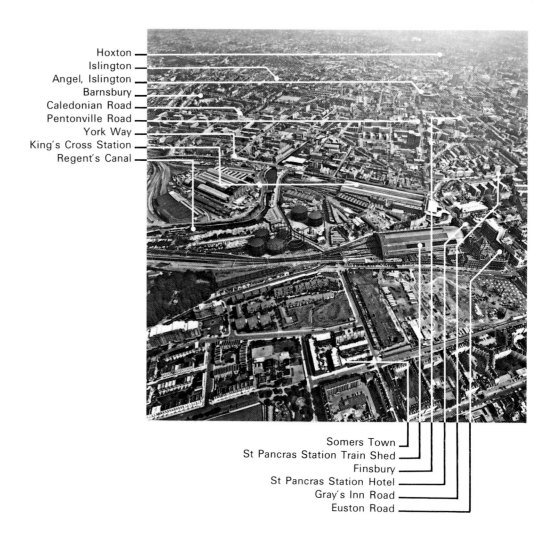

Hoxton —
Islington —
Angel, Islington —
Barnsbury —
Caledonian Road —
Pentonville Road —
York Way —
King's Cross Station —
Regent's Canal —

Somers Town
St Pancras Station Train Shed
Finsbury
St Pancras Station Hotel
Gray's Inn Road
Euston Road

ST PANCRAS

We are now a little to the south and east of the last picture and come to the two most interesting stations in London. St Pancras indeed is more than a station, for the front of it consisted of an enormous and ultra-luxurious hotel. The actual train shed of the station (1868) is by W.H. Barlow and R.M. Ordish, and they gave it unrivalled dimensions – nearly 700 feet in length and 240 wide. At the same time Sir George Gilbert Scott was asked to provide the façade and hotel. Palmerston had not allowed him to do the new Foreign Office in Gothic, so he now used the wasted expertise to produce a brick Gothic fantasy which makes Street's Law Courts seem sedate and rivals even Barry's Houses of Parliament. Nevertheless, in the late 1960s prodigies of public agitation were required to prevent British Rail pulling down this

masterpiece, as it had earlier demolished the magnificent classical front of Euston. King's Cross Station nearby is in total contrast. Many people think its twin arch, which functionally reflects the two great iron sheds behind it, is modern. In fact, Lewis and Joseph Cubitt designed it in 1851, fifteen years before St Pancras was thought of, though it is certainly modern in spirit. These two great designs, side by side, give the lie to the notion that the Victorians all thought alike. Far more uniform, in fact, are the post-war housing estates off the Caledonian Road, the Pentonville Road and the Gray's Inn Road. Meanwhile, the Regent's Canal continues to wander south-eastwards, and when it crosses under York Way it takes us into Islington and especially Barnsbury, with its elegant crescents, terraces and squares.

126

Camden Town
Regent's Park
Euston Station
Fitzroy Square

Euston Road
Gordon Square
Tavistock Square
Brunswick Square
Russell Square

Coram's Fields
Gray's Inn Road
Great Ormond Street

Times Newspapers
St Pancras Station
King's Cross Station
Pentonville Road

BLOOMSBURY

'Our part of London is so very superior to most others. You must not confound us with London in general, my dear Sir'. Not Virginia Woolf, actually, or any of the Bloomsberries, but Isabella in Jane Austen's *Emma*, extolling the healthy properties of Brunswick Square. But Virginia did live there, at number 38, which she shared with J.M. Keynes, Duncan Grant and Leonard Woolf. *Quelle galère*! Earlier she had lived at 29 Fitzroy Square, further west. The main centre of the Bloomsbury Group, however, was Gordon Square, in among the London University Buildings, where consorted E.M. Forster, Roger Fry, Lytton Strachey and G.E. Moore, as well as the others. Number 51 was Strachey's couch. Other Bloomsbury Group *foci* were 3 Gower Street, 10 Great Ormond Street and 52 Tavistock Square. Strictly speaking, Bloomsbury is bounded by Tottenham Court Road on the

west, Euston Road on the north, Gray's Inn Road on the east and Theobald's Road on the south. The Fitzroy Square-Charlotte Street zone is more properly termed Fitzrovia, or even North Soho. In our picture the Gray's Inn Road, cutting diagonally across the bottom half, with the new Times Newspaper building at the bottom, divides Bloomsbury from Clerkenwell. Coram's Fields takes up the centre, with the trees of Russell Square to the left. This picture is taken from the reverse direction of the one on the previous pages, so we get a good view of the twin façades of St Pancras and King's Cross. To the left, beyond the tall glass tower of the Euston Centre, we see the full extent of Regent's Park. As Virginia Woolf put it herself in *Mrs Dalloway*: 'Life itself, every moment of it, every drop of it, here, this instant, now, in the sun, in Regent's Park, was enough. Too much, indeed.'

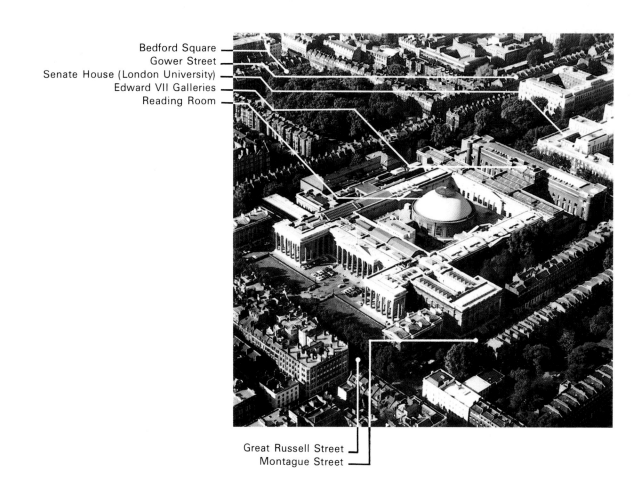

Bedford Square
Gower Street
Senate House (London University)
Edward VII Galleries
Reading Room

Great Russell Street
Montague Street

THE BRITISH MUSEUM

'Manuscripts and rarities by the cart-load', wrote the poet Thomas Gray in 1759, describing the opening of the British Museum. This was Montague House, purchased to display the vast collections of Sir Hans Soane and the Harleian and Cottonian Manuscripts, all presented to the nation. Later came the Elgin Marbles and the Rosetta Stone from Egypt. When George IV donated his father's vast collection of books, Sir Robert Smirke was chosen to design a wing, the King's Library, behind the existing galleries. With the further expansion of the collections, Montague House was pulled down and replaced by Smirke's marvellous classical façade, which was completed in the 1840s. The buildings now formed a vast open quadrangle. In the next decade, to accommodate the ever-growing national book collection,

the Keeper of Printed Books, Anthony Panizzi, roofed in the quadrangle and crowned it with an enormous dome; beneath it he created the world's most inspiring reading room, in which Karl Marx plotted the destruction of the civilization which had produced it. There are now plans to take it, along with the books, to a site at St Pancras where work has already started; but they are being resisted, for no other building on earth contains side-by-side so rich a collection of both art and literature. To quote Virginia Woolf again, 'There is in the British Museum an enormous mind. Consider that Plato is there cheek by jowl with Aristotle; and Shakespeare with Marlowe. This great mind is hoarded beyond the power of any single mind to possess it.' Or, one might add, to remove it from its present superb home.

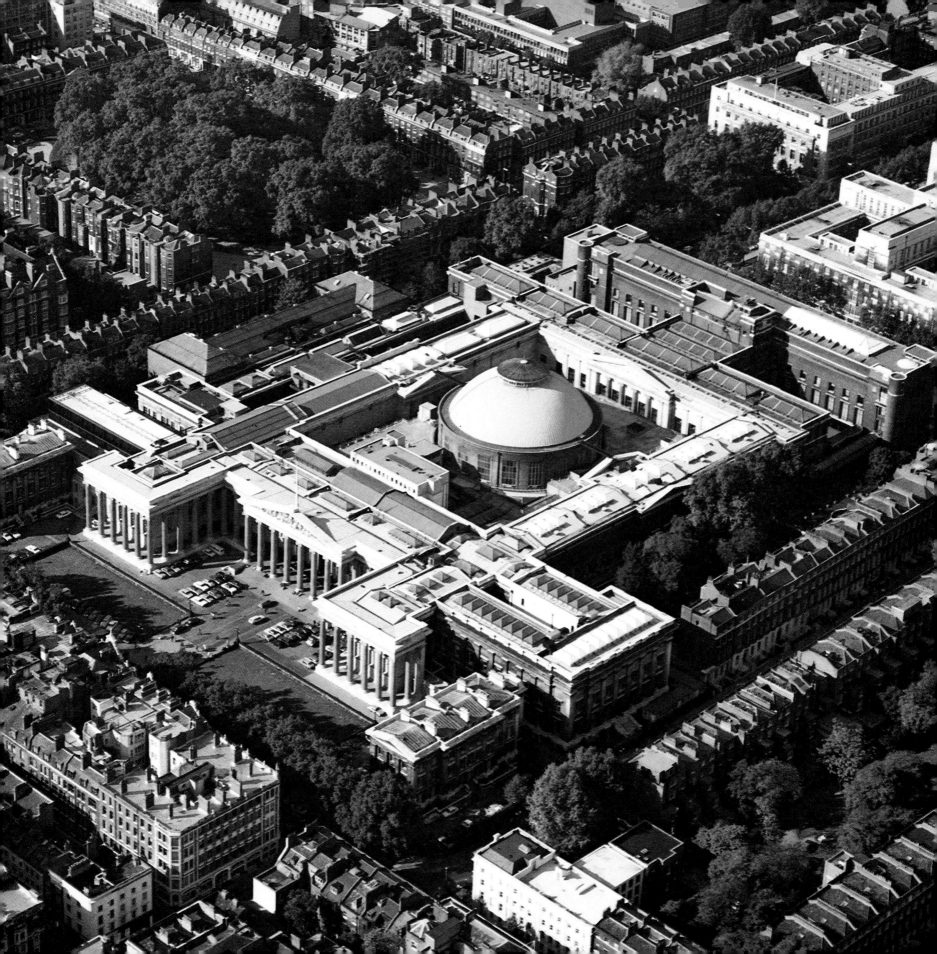

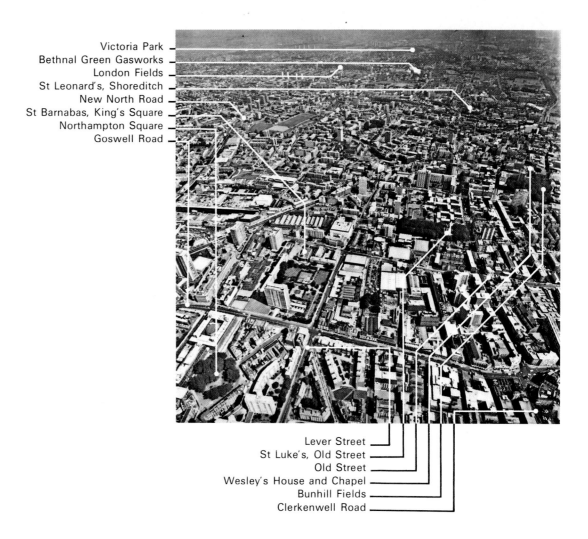

Victoria Park —
Bethnal Green Gasworks —
London Fields —
St Leonard's, Shoreditch —
New North Road —
St Barnabas, King's Square —
Northampton Square —
Goswell Road —

Lever Street ———
St Luke's, Old Street ———
Old Street ———
Wesley's House and Chapel ———
Bunhill Fields ———
Clerkenwell Road ———

CLERKENWELL

Making sense of this huge stretch of north-east London is not easy. The best way, as before, is to follow the Regent's Canal, which enters the picture left-centre in Islington, moves under the New North Road through Shoreditch, under Kingsland Road through Haggerston, then with the green of London Fields on its left, and Bethnal Green Gasworks on its right, skirts the trees of Victoria Park and passes out of the picture top right on its way to the Thames. In the left foreground are the trees of Northampton Square, with the brash new buildings of the City University. Lever Street runs from the bottom into the middle of the picture, where it merges with City Road coming in from the centre left. Goswell Road runs from left to right across the bottom of the picture, crossing Clerkenwell Road, which joins City Road at the circus where once stood St Agnes's Well. Not much to look at in this

district, I fear, though there are three pretty churches. St Barnabas, King's Square (1826), by Thomas Hardwick, is just left of Lever Street near the centre of the picture; and the famous obelisk spire of St Luke's is left of Old Street, peering out from amongst its trees. Another obelisk-spire church, on a much grander scale, is just visible in the top right-hand corner: George Dance the Elder's St Leonard (1736), the parish church of Shoreditch. It is nearly 200 feet tall and sticks out even in this indeterminate neighbourhood of sawn-off skyscrapers and council tower-blocks. Almost but not quite invisible on the City Road (right-centre of the picture) opposite the green of Bunhill Fields, the famous nonconformist cemetery, is Wesley's Chapel (1777), with his statue in front and his grave behind it.

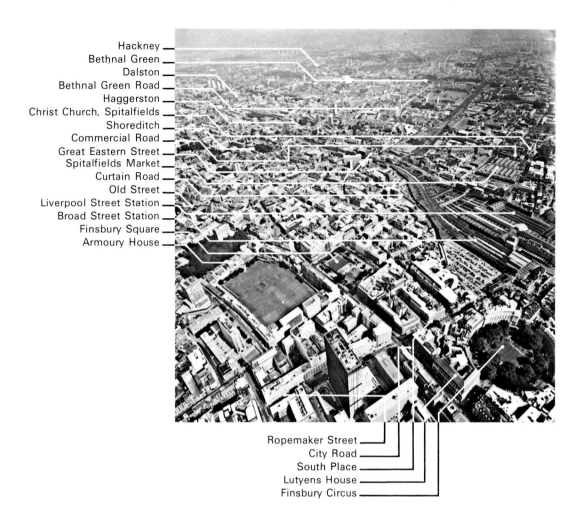

Hackney
Bethnal Green
Dalston
Bethnal Green Road
Haggerston
Christ Church, Spitalfields
Shoreditch
Commercial Road
Great Eastern Street
Spitalfields Market
Curtain Road
Old Street
Liverpool Street Station
Broad Street Station
Finsbury Square
Armoury House

Ropemaker Street
City Road
South Place
Lutyens House
Finsbury Circus

SHOREDITCH

Apart from the Tower itself, this is the most 'military' part of London. The defence perimeter of the London Wall ran just out of our picture at the bottom, and this section contained the great barbican, the most powerful fortification in all north London. The area was badly bombed in the war and has now been replaced by the 60-acre Barbican scheme, which includes permanent homes for the Royal Shakespeare Company and the London Symphony Orchestra, the magnificent new London Museum, and flats for 6,000 people. The Moorgate in the Wall led into City Road, running across the bottom of the picture, and what we are looking at are the Moorfields, once a region of open, marshy country. Henry VIII used to go hawking and wildfowling here, but it was also used for archery and shooting practice. In 1537 he gave a corporate charter to the Honourable Artillery Company, which thus became England's oldest regiment. The big field off City Road is still its parade and practice ground (it was also used for England's first balloon ascent in 1784). At the top is Armoury House, its HQ, with its

'Golden Book' containing signatures of all its members, including Milton, Pepys and Wren. As this region was outside the City limits it attracted activities forbidden within them, such as theatres. James Burbage built a theatre in Shoreditch in 1576 and another, the Curtain, opened in Curtain Road the next year. Refugees from the Continent also arrived here in growing numbers. French Huguenots settled just to the east of what is now Liverpool Street Station, around Spitalfields Market. Spital, of course, is a contraction of 'Hospital': there were many in this area, of which the most famous survivor is the Moorfields Eye Hospital at the bottom of the picture. Opposite is Finsbury Circus with its bowling green and a majestic building by Sir Edwin Lutyens. But attempts to beautify this part of London have not lasted. Finsbury Square, laid out by George Dance the Younger in 1777, has all been replaced by business clutter. City Mammon is too near.

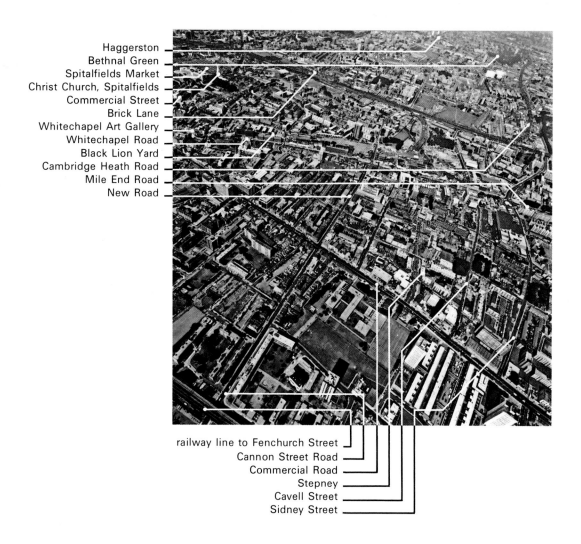

Haggerston
Bethnal Green
Spitalfields Market
Christ Church, Spitalfields
Commercial Street
Brick Lane
Whitechapel Art Gallery
Whitechapel Road
Black Lion Yard
Cambridge Heath Road
Mile End Road
New Road

railway line to Fenchurch Street
Cannon Street Road
Commercial Road
Stepney
Cavell Street
Sidney Street

JACK THE RIPPER'S LONDON

Between the Liverpool Street Station main line and the Commercial Road, that is, either side of the Whitechapel-Mile End Road, is the traditional East End of London, as it existed from the early nineteenth century to the Second World War. It might be termed 'Jack the Ripper's London'. He struck first in Gunthorpe Street, just off the Whitechapel Road near Aldgate East tube station, on 2 April 1888. Eight more murders followed over the next eighteen months, all of them in or off the Commercial Road. The victims were prostitutes, what Queen Victoria termed 'unfortunate women of a bad class'. The bodies were mutilated by what appeared to be a skilful hand. The Queen, like most other people, was fascinated by 'these dreadful murders'. Her alleged spiritualist mentor, Robert Lees, claimed to have identified the monster, during a seance, as a crazed Harley Street doctor and to have recognized him on a bus in Notting Hill. But no

arrest was ever made. All the ghosts and mysteries of the East End were expelled by the German blitz, for as John Aubrey put it, 'gunpowder is a great fugator of phantoms'. Post-war reconstruction has been particularly bitty and unimpressive here. A few of the old terraces remain off Fordham Street, between the Whitechapel and Commercial Roads, though more interesting are the façades of the old shops along the Whitechapel Road, especially the stretch between New Road and Cambridge Heath Road. Here is Cockney London as it once was. The area was famous for breweries, silversmiths, small foundries and slaughterhouses. Of the last, there is still a famous kosher one in Cobb Street, while in Black Lion Yard silversmiths flourish even now. Another survivor is the Whitechapel Bell Foundry, which has been casting bells for City churches and Westminster Abbey since the sixteenth century.

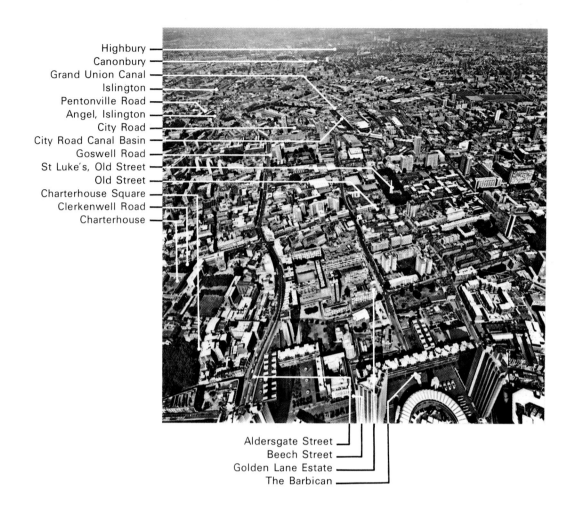

Highbury
Canonbury
Grand Union Canal
Islington
Pentonville Road
Angel, Islington
City Road
City Road Canal Basin
Goswell Road
St Luke's, Old Street
Old Street
Charterhouse Square
Clerkenwell Road
Charterhouse

Aldersgate Street
Beech Street
Golden Lane Estate
The Barbican

ALDERSGATE

We are now on the northern edge of the City. In fact the boundary runs along a jagged line north of Beech Street at the bottom of our photograph. The enormous Barbican development is just inside the City line, and we look down on two of its three tower-blocks, which with 44 storeys and a height of well over 400 feet are the tallest flats in Britain. Beyond the boundary is the so-called North Barbican or Golden Lane Estate, built in the late Fifties and early Sixties with a tower-block (including a decorative 'butterfly-wing' water tank) which looks timid by comparison. Also outside the City, to the left of Aldersgate Street, is the Charterhouse. This is not only one of the most important medieval survivals in London – the cloister of the Carthusian Priory, founded 1371, is on the left of the picture – but also the only remaining example of a grand Tudor town house. After Henry VIII broke up the priory he gave its buildings to his courtier Lord

North, and thence it passed to the fourth Duke of Norfolk, who embellished it luxuriously. Alas, he plotted against Queen Elizabeth with Mary Queen of Scots, exchanging cipher letters; and one of his secretaries, on the rack, confessed that the key to the cipher was in the Charterhouse, 'under a mat, hard by the window's side, where the map of England doth hang'. It was actually found under a tile in the roof, and that did for the Duke, executed in the Tower in 1572. In James I's day, Thomas Sutton turned it into an almshouse for distressed gentry, with a school attached. Thackeray went to Charterhouse and described it all in *The Newcomes*. From 1875 to 1933 it was the Merchant Taylors' School, but it is now the medical school of St Bartholomew's Hospital, who have added modern extensions on the right: a typical example of the multiple usages to which a historical London site has been put.

138

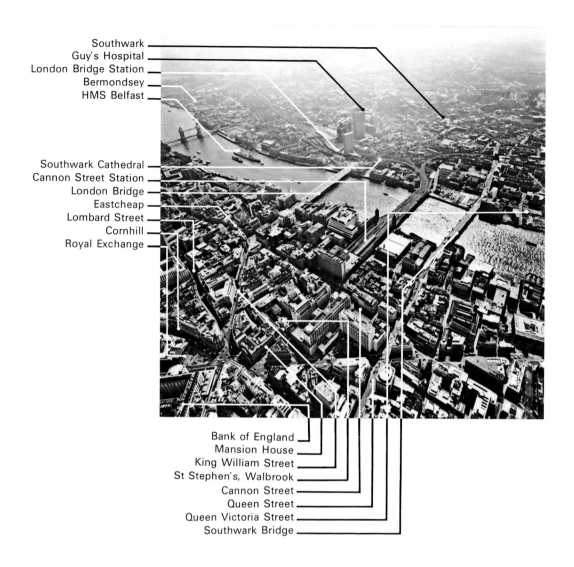

Southwark
Guy's Hospital
London Bridge Station
Bermondsey
HMS Belfast

Southwark Cathedral
Cannon Street Station
London Bridge
Eastcheap
Lombard Street
Cornhill
Royal Exchange

Bank of England
Mansion House
King William Street
St Stephen's, Walbrook
Cannon Street
Queen Street
Queen Victoria Street
Southwark Bridge

THE LONDON OF MAMMON

This has always been the heart of London. In Roman times the Palace and Temple were behind Cannon Street Station, the Forum behind London Bridge. Virtually all the street names reflect the fact that this was a buying and selling area, first in Roman, then medieval times. Fenchurch Street is from *faenum*, hay. The Corn Market was on Cornmarket Street. Candles were sold on Candlewick (now Cannon) Street. The main market street derives from Saxon *ceap*, to sell, and was divided into Westcheap (now Cheapside) and Eastcheap. Lombard Street got its name in the late fourteenth century when Italians replaced the Jewish money-changers and bankers in what was already the financial centre of the city, where eight of its chief streets met. Then, in 1566, the great Elizabethan financier Sir Thomas Gresham built England's first Exchange, modelled on Antwerp's, where merchants could barter. The present building, late classical revival of the 1840s, is by Sir William Tite. Next to it is the Bank of England, founded in 1694. The enormous building, covering three acres, was by Sir John Soane, built over the years 1788–1808. Between the wars all but the façade was knocked down by Sir Herbert Baker and filled in to provide more office space. Opposite is the Mansion House, the official residence of the Lord Mayor, built in the mid-eighteenth century by George Dance the Elder. Just behind it, in Walbrook (derived from the stream which provided the water supply of Roman and early medieval London), is St Stephen's, rebuilt by Wren in the 1670s, with a pretty little spire and, more significantly, a marvellous dome, which is close to his original design for St Paul's.

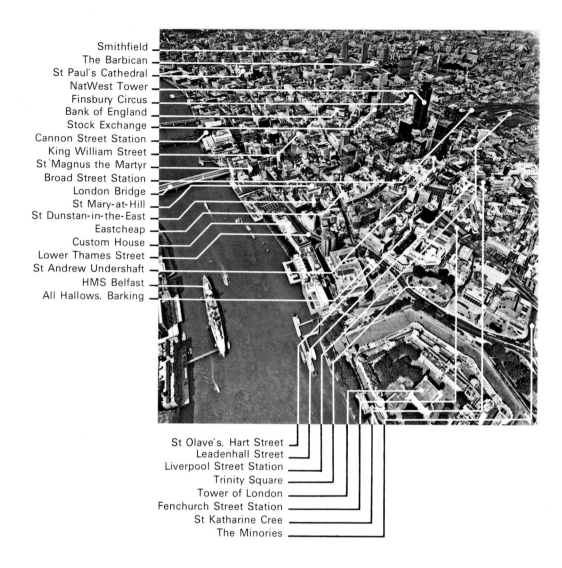

Smithfield
The Barbican
St Paul's Cathedral
NatWest Tower
Finsbury Circus
Bank of England
Stock Exchange
Cannon Street Station
King William Street
St Magnus the Martyr
Broad Street Station
London Bridge
St Mary-at-Hill
St Dunstan-in-the-East
Eastcheap
Custom House
Lower Thames Street
St Andrew Undershaft
HMS Belfast
All Hallows, Barking

St Olave's, Hart Street
Leadenhall Street
Liverpool Street Station
Trinity Square
Tower of London
Fenchurch Street Station
St Katharine Cree
The Minories

THE CITY

This picture allows one to see almost the entire City of London at a glance, and to trace its boundaries in detail. The City boundary starts on the river west of the Tower, runs on the far side of Trinity Square, up the Minories (called after the Minoresses or Poor Clare nuns), takes in Liverpool Street Station on the top right, includes Finsbury Circus, visible behind the black outline of the NatWest Tower, then goes behind the Barbican, with its vast slab and three towers, includes the long flat roof of Smithfield, and then plunges due south on the far side of St Paul's to hit the river at Blackfriars Bridge, just off the top left-hand corner of the picture. The medieval city had about 20,000 living in it at the end of the fourteenth century. By 1600 it had risen to around 100,000 and by 1700 to perhaps as many as 140,000. By then the movement to the suburbs had begun. By 1801 only 128,000 people lived actually in the City; by 1861, 112,000. By the 1880s only 50,000

lived there, and in the 1950s it fell as low as 5,000. Today, despite the Barbican development, it is not much over 10,000. That poses many problems of upkeep, especially for the City's vast collection of churches. Here are just a few which can be seen from this angle: All Hallows Barking (Great Tower Street), medieval and mid-seventeenth century; St Dunstan-in-the East by Wren (1679), just behind the Customs House; St Magnus the Martyr by Wren (1671) in Lower Thames Street; St Mary-at-Hill by Wren (1670) just below Eastcheap; St Olave's, Hart Street (medieval) below Fenchurch Street Station; and on Leadenhall Street St Katharine Cree (1628) and St Andrew Undershaft (fifteenth and sixteenth century). I have spotted sixteen other City churches in this photograph (not of course counting St Paul's), peeping in and out of the skyscraper banks and office-blocks. Who said there is no room for both God and Mammon?

Limehouse
Tower of London
Mincing Lane
Whitechapel
Fenchurch Street
Gracechurch Street
Spitalfields
St Peter upon Cornhill
NatWest Tower
Lombard Street
St Michael's, Cornhill
St Botolph's
Liverpool Street Station
Bishopsgate
Old Broad Street
All Hallows, London Wall
London Wall
Finsbury Circus

Throgmorton Street
Stock Exchange
Bank of England
Threadneedle Street
Globe Insurance
Midland Bank
Cornhill
St Edmund the King

SCROOGE'S LONDON

Here we are looking at the central part of the City financial district from the other side, that is the west. Bottom right is the triangle of the Bank of England, with the dome of the Globe Insurance building on the corner of Cornhill and Lombard Street. At the top of Lombard Street is Hawksmoor's St Mary Woolnoth (1716), and further down on the left-hand side St Edmund-the-King by Wren (1670), almost opposite which was Change Alley, scene of the wild South Sea Bubble speculation. After Lombard Street comes Fenchurch Street, and Mincing Lane on the right (called after the nuns of St Helen's convent) marks the headquarters of the tea trade. Down Cornhill, on the right, is St Michael's, in which both Wren and Hawksmoor had a hand, though the gleaming Gothic tower was the work of Sir George Gilbert Scott in the 1850s. St Michael's Alley was the site of the City's first coffee house. Behind the Bank, sandwiched between Threadneedle

Street and Throgmorton Street, is the new Stock Exchange, with its great concourse and skyscraper, and beyond it Old Broad Street with its Dutch Church opposite the high NatWest Tower. On the far side of this tower Bishopsgate runs down from Liverpool Street Station on the left into Gracechurch Street and so to London Bridge. Near the station on Bishopsgate is St Botolph's, rebuilt from its medieval foundations in the 1720s by James Gould and George Dance the Elder. Then, coming back towards us on the straight line of London Wall is the little church of All Hallows, designed in 1765 by Dance's son, George Dance the Younger, when he was only twenty-four. He was also responsible for Finsbury Circus, to the left, an idea he conceived in 1802. It's odd to think that City magnates once lived in these grand houses, though needless to say none of the originals remains and all is now office space.

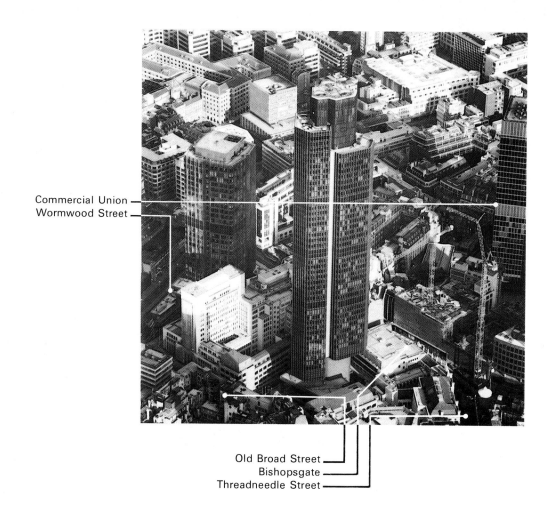

Commercial Union —
Wormwood Street —

Old Broad Street —
Bishopsgate —
Threadneedle Street —

THE NATWEST TOWER

If the National Westminster Bank's great tower already has a slightly dated look, in terms of rapidly changing skyscraper fashions, it might be explained by the long period of gestation a project of this kind needs. Most of the Bishopsgate-Old Broad Street site had been acquired over more than a century; the final piece in the jigsaw fitted when National Provincial (the core of NatWest) bought Gresham House in 1959. Outline planning permission for a tower was granted in November 1964. Construction began in March 1971 and was completed ten years later (the tower itself was 'topped out' in 1977). With 52 floors and 600 feet in height, it is Britain's tallest office building, and from the top it is possible to see seven counties: Berkshire, Buckinghamshire, Hert-

fordshire, Essex, Kent, Sussex and Surrey. About 2,500 people work there, going up and down in 21 lifts which can travel at 1,400 feet a minute. Physically, the tower dominates the eastern part of the City in the way St Paul's once dominated the whole. It links up with Centre Point at the east end of Oxford Street, and the Hilton Hotel at the bottom of Park Lane, to form a trio of orienting points of reference covering nearly all London. But it is best seen from above or afar; from ground level it is too hemmed in by neighbouring clutter to make the impression its height deserves. Its site is only just north of the original Roman market place and illustrates the extraordinary geographical continuity of London's commercial core.

Museum of London
Gresham Street
Bloomsbury
Finsbury
Clerkenwell
Smithfield
Holborn Viaduct
Lincoln's Inn Fields
Holborn Viaduct Station
Royal Courts of Justice
Newgate Street
Farringdon Street
Fleet Street
Central Criminal Court
Ludgate Circus
St Martin's, Ludgate Hill
Stationers' Hall
Ludgate Hill
Carter Lane
The Deanery
Unilever House
Apothecaries' Hall
Faraday House
Blackfriars Station
Mermaid Theatre

Cutlers' Hall
Paternoster Square
St Benet's, Paul's Wharf
Chapter House
St Paul's Cathedral
Queen Victoria Street
St Martin's-le-Grand
St Paul's Choir School

MERCANTILE LONDON

This is the western end of the City, with its old limit at Temple Bar just out of sight beyond the Law Courts at the left-centre of the picture. From there Fleet Street goes east, over Ludgate Circus and up Ludgate Hill to St Paul's. All this area was badly bombed by the Germans. The old London publishing quarter around St Paul's was wiped out, never to return. Most of the old City guild-halls were destroyed or damaged; but they at least have been rebuilt. Six can be seen here. Stationers' Hall is north of Ludgate Hill behind Wren's St Martin's, Ludgate Hill (1677). Below it in Blackfriars Lane is the Apothecaries' Hall. On Warwick Lane, running south of Newgate, is the Cutlers' Hall. Behind St Paul's there is the Goldsmiths' Hall on Gresham Street, and on either side of the London Museum in the new Barbican development are the Ironmongers and the Plasterers. Next to the Cutlers' Hall is the Central Criminal Court (Old Bailey) with its

dome and blind justice holding sword and scales, and further along Newgate Street is the huge development of Paternoster Square, designed by Lord Holford, which was put up in the 1960s. Hard to conceive of anything less congruous with St Paul's than these blocks and slabs, though it is true they are faced with the same Portland stone as the cathedral. The most westerly one alters the famous view of St Paul's west front up Ludgate Hill. What St Paul's has always lacked is a proper precinct. Wren's Chapter House is on the north of the cathedral, now muddled up with Holford's blocks. The Deanery, possibly also by Wren, is buried in the huddled alleys to the south. There is a post-war garden on the south-east side but it lacks repose. In short the surroundings of the St Paul's are unhelpful, to put it mildly. It has to stand on its own merits. Fortunately they are considerable.

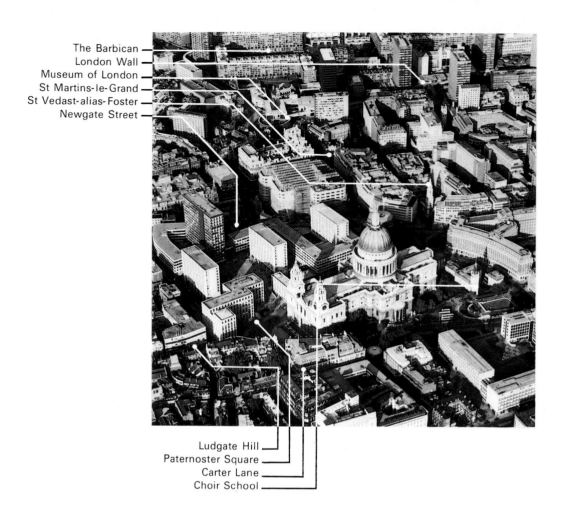

The Barbican
London Wall
Museum of London
St Martins-le-Grand
St Vedast-alias-Foster
Newgate Street

Ludgate Hill
Paternoster Square
Carter Lane
Choir School

ST PAUL'S CATHEDRAL

The Great Fire of 1666 gave Wren, one of the new gentleman-architects who had replaced the old medieval master-builders, the chance to create a major cathedral blending baroque and classical. But the ground-plan is the typically English cruciform, with all the parts – chancel, navel, crossing, transepts – quite distinct; the long nave recalls English Gothic cathedrals, and the west front, with towers placed outside the aisles, is also English. The story of Wren's battles to get the great church built is almost as monumental as the structure itself. The first stone of the chancel was laid in 1675; work reached the transepts in 1681; the nave was started in 1684, the west front in 1686. It was consecrated in 1697, the west towers finished in 1708, the dome in 1710. Wren had to fight tiresome committees all the way, and was badly paid; as the Duchess of Marlborough put it, he 'allowed himself to be dragged up in a basket to the top of the scaffolding, two or three times a week to the hazard of his life, for a paltry £200 a year'. In 1718,

aged eighty-six, he was sacked, and the next year, against his express wishes, an open stone balustrade was added round the top of the building, evoking his contemptuous comment: 'Ladies think nothing well without an edging'. But at least, unlike the medieval cathedral-builders, he lived to see his work finished. Until his death in 1723, he travelled up once a year from his house in Hampton Court, to sit under his dome for an hour, in silence. Old St Paul's, on its hill, had dominated the medieval city; Wren's St Paul's dominated the baroque and classical city which replaced it after the fire. His hand was on it all, for he designed no fewer than 51 new churches in the City (plus three outside it), 17 in the single year 1670. St Paul's and 23 of the churches remain, but what Wren could not have foreseen is the extent to which his enormous cathedral would be masked and even dwarfed by the steel-and-concrete commercial monsters of the twentieth century.

Farringdon Road
Holborn Viaduct
Farringdon Underground Station
General Market
Poultry Market
Meat Market
West Smithfield
St Bartholomew the Great
St Bartholomew's Hospital
Little Britain

SMITHFIELD

Smithfield meant 'smoothfield' or grass open space. It was used for all kinds of crowd activities, notably tournaments and executions. Edward I executed the Scots patriot William Wallace here in 1305, and the Mayor cut down Wat Tyler, in front of Richard II, in 1381; in the 1550s Queen Mary burnt Protestants. There are memorials to such victims on the walls of St Bartholomew's Hospital, below the circus. But Smithfield was chiefly famous for its St Bartholomew's Fair and its enormous meat market. The cattle were driven in on the hoof and, after purchase, slaughtered in the Newgate 'shambles' on the other side of the hospital. The area was thought disgusting by the Victorians, so the cattle market was shifted to Copenhagen Fields in 1855 and the Shambles abolished by parliament six years later. The coming of the Metropolitan Railway permitted an ingenious solution: the trains unloaded the meat carcasses on to underground platforms, and above

them Sir Horace Jones designed a splendid enclosed market with cupolas at the corners. It opened in 1868 with a banquet for 1,200 City grandees, who consumed boars' heads and barons of beef, and toasted 'Tolls to the Corporation, cheap meat to the people, and profits to the salesmen'. Half Smithfield was knocked down in the war and rebuilt; so it now consists of the meat market proper (the original), the new poultry market (1960s) with a 225-foot clear-span roof; and the old General Market with a pretty dome in the middle. The trains have gone, and underneath there is now a gigantic car park. The market is open five days a week from midnight, when 'pitchers' begin to unload the carcasses, using the 'Smithfield Shuffle' or trot. Trading begins at five a.m. and is finished by eight a.m. By midday all is tidy, clean and clear.

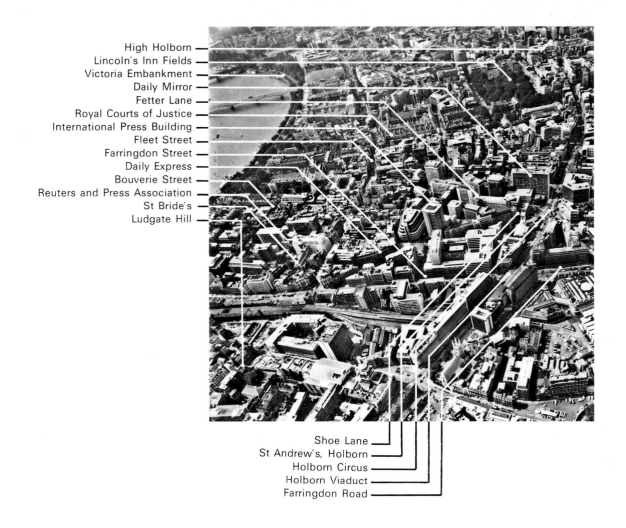

High Holborn —
Lincoln's Inn Fields —
Victoria Embankment —
Daily Mirror —
Fetter Lane —
Royal Courts of Justice —
International Press Building —
Fleet Street —
Farringdon Street —
Daily Express —
Bouverie Street —
Reuters and Press Association —
St Bride's —
Ludgate Hill —

Shoe Lane ——
St Andrew's, Holborn ——
Holborn Circus ——
Holborn Viaduct ——
Farringdon Road ——

FLEET STREET

In the eighteenth century, the stationery trade gradually spread from St Paul's down Ludgate Hill and into Fleet Street. Farringdon Road was once a deep ravine dividing St Paul's from the western outskirts of the City, and in the 1860s the Corporation got their Surveyor, William Haywood, to build a magnificent cast-iron bridge, called Holborn Viaduct, thus taking Newgate Street smoothly into High Holborn. Holborn Circus, just in front of Wren's pretty church of St Andrew (1684) is the best place to survey Journalists' London. To the right, up Farringdon Road, is the *Guardian*. *The Times*, once directly underneath St Paul's in Printing House Square (the *Observer* is still there on St Andrew's Hill), is just off the picture, together with the *Sunday Times*, up the Gray's Inn Road. Just down Holborn, in a red skyscraper slab, is the Mirror Group: the *Daily* and *Sunday Mirror*, *People* and *Sporting Life*. Below Holborn Circus, down Shoe Lane, is the skyscraper of the International Press Building, housing much of the foreign press, and at the bottom of it, on the south side of Fleet Street itself, is the gleaming stonework of the magnificent headquarters Lutyens designed for Reuters and the Press Association in 1935. Opposite, but seen from the rear, is the revolutionary black glass building (1931) which houses the *Daily* and *Sunday Express* and the *Standard*. Further up on the same side (again seen from the back) are the *Daily* and *Sunday Telegraph*. Two poky lanes lead off Fleet Street to the south: down Whitefriars' Street are the *Daily Mail* and *Mail on Sunday*; down Bouverie Street are the *Sun* and *News of the World*. For liquid refreshments journalists go to El Vino's on Fleet Street opposite the bottom of Fetter Lane, and for spiritual comfort to Wren's magnificent St Bride's (1671), with its 226-foot spire, next to Reuters.

154

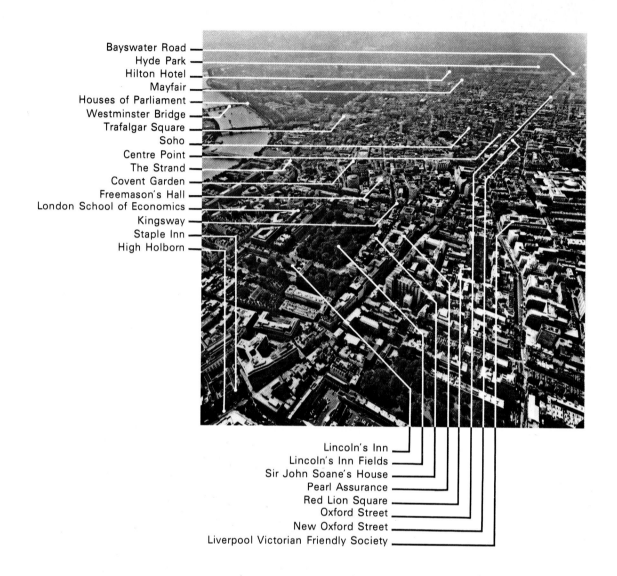

Bayswater Road
Hyde Park
Hilton Hotel
Mayfair
Houses of Parliament
Westminster Bridge
Trafalgar Square
Soho
Centre Point
The Strand
Covent Garden
Freemason's Hall
London School of Economics
Kingsway
Staple Inn
High Holborn

Lincoln's Inn
Lincoln's Inn Fields
Sir John Soane's House
Pearl Assurance
Red Lion Square
Oxford Street
New Oxford Street
Liverpool Victorian Friendly Society

HOLBORN

Here we have most of west London as seen from the edge of the City at a point above Gray's Inn Road. What is most striking is the continuous axis of London's main road to the west, beginning as Cheapside in the City heart, then becoming in turn Newgate Street, Holborn, High Holborn, New Oxford Street, Oxford Street and then, when it hits the north side of Hyde Park at the top right-hand corner of the picture, Bayswater, running into Shepherd's Bush. The whole stretch we see across the picture is about four miles. There is a lot to describe. In the bottom left-hand corner, on the south side of Holborn and fronting old Staple Inn, is the best, almost the only, group of Elizabethan half-timbered houses in London. Opposite, just out of the picture, is Alfred Waterhouse's superb red-brick Prudential Building. Indeed, this is insurers' London, with the Pearl Assurance building (1912) and its pretty cupola further up Holborn, and the Liverpool Victoria Friendly Society building in Southampton Row. What stands out is

the green of Gray's Inn gardens in the foreground, Red Lion Square above it and, most of all, Lincoln's Inn Fields. This is not only the biggest square in central London but the earliest (if we except Covent Garden), having been laid out by Inigo Jones before the Civil War, in imitation of the new Place des Vosges in Paris. All but one of Jones's houses have gone but George Dance the Younger's magnificent Royal College of Surgeons (who now have a new building in Regent's Park) is on the south side, while on the north is the brilliantly innovatory house built for himself by the designer of the Bank of England, Sir John Soane, which now houses his collections. Other striking buildings in this picture are the Silver Vaults on Chancery Lane, the London School of Economics behind the south-west corner of the Fields, and beyond Kingsway the huge block of Freemasons' Hall (1931), headquarters of British masons. Centre Point and the Hilton Hotel stand out as always, the first overshadowing Soho, the second Mayfair.

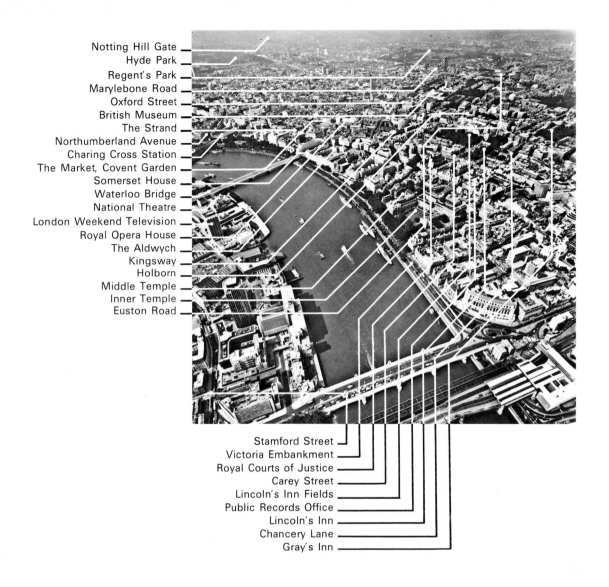

Notting Hill Gate —
Hyde Park —
Regent's Park —
Marylebone Road —
Oxford Street —
British Museum —
The Strand —
Northumberland Avenue —
Charing Cross Station —
The Market, Covent Garden —
Somerset House —
Waterloo Bridge —
National Theatre —
London Weekend Television —
Royal Opera House —
The Aldwych —
Kingsway —
Holborn —
Middle Temple —
Inner Temple —
Euston Road —

Stamford Street —
Victoria Embankment —
Royal Courts of Justice —
Carey Street —
Lincoln's Inn Fields —
Public Records Office —
Lincoln's Inn —
Chancery Lane —
Gray's Inn —

LAWYERS' LONDON

Before it was banked the Thames could be a nuisance, flooding in the winter and often leaving patches of stagnant river-bed exposed in summer. Wren wanted to bank the whole stretch from Westminster to Blackfriars but nothing was done until the 1860s, when Sir Joseph Bazalgette put up the Victoria Embankment, creating a series of gardens in the process. North of it lies Lawyers' London, formed by the series of societies of Inns that medieval pleaders formed outside the City limits but on the route to the main law courts at Westminster. Four Inns taught the Common Law: the Inner and Middle Temple between Temple Gardens and Fleet Street; Lincoln's Inn, whose green patch can be seen between Chancery Lane and Lincoln's Inn Fields; and Gray's Inn, almost out of the picture on the top right. There were also nine smaller Inns teaching the Continental-style equity practised in the Lord Chancellor's court. Three have com-

pletely disappeared and four survive only as names of modern buildings, but the Staple Inn off Holborn, Barnard's Inn and Sergeant's Inn off Fleet Street have a vestigial existence. In early modern times Chancery shifted from Westminster to Lincoln's Inn, and then in the 1870s settled in the new Royal Courts of Justice designed in fantasy Gothic by G.E. Street, at the point where the Strand becomes Fleet Street. Behind it is Carey Street, where people go to be made bankrupt, and behind that the Central Land Registry on Lincoln's Inn Fields. On Chancery Lane, just to the east, is the domain of the Master of the Rolls, who is still technically responsible for the Public Records Office. Opposite this is the Law Society, headquarters of the soliciting profession, whose president occupies a beautiful eighteenth-century house just round the corner in Carey Street. Dickens describes this region hauntingly in *Bleak House*.

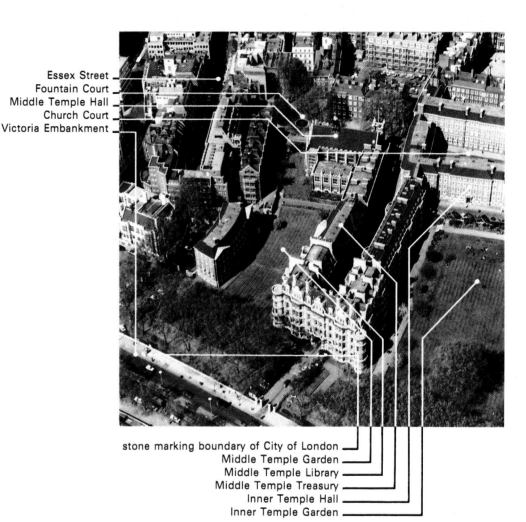

Essex Street
Fountain Court
Middle Temple Hall
Church Court
Victoria Embankment

stone marking boundary of City of London
Middle Temple Garden
Middle Temple Library
Middle Temple Treasury
Inner Temple Hall
Inner Temple Garden

THE TEMPLE

The two richest and most famous Inns, the Inner and Middle Temple, are built over the twelfth-century headquarters of the English Poor Knights of Christ and Solomon's Temple. They were privileged to have round churches, like that of the Holy Sepulchre, and London's Temple Church is one of only four circular medieval churches in the country. The trouble with the knights was that they were not poor, but very rich; so they were suppressed and robbed by the Crown in the early fourteenth century, and the Inns grew up on their property. Here, in the Temple Garden, according to Shakespeare (Henry VI, Part One), the Wars of the Roses began, with each side plucking different coloured roses. There is some kind of war between the two Inns, since their evolution into separate establishments occurred very early and each jealously preserves its independence of the other, though there is no obvious visible distinction between the two. The best way in is through the arch in Middle Temple Lane, where Dr

Johnson once had a set of rooms. The atmosphere is collegiate, as at Oxford or Cambridge, with barristers grouped together in 'chambers' on separate staircases, exactly as in an Oxbridge College. Most of these are eighteenth-century; indeed, the Temple has some of the finest Georgian houses in London, especially on King's Bench Walk. But the place was badly battered during the last war and the new buildings are undistinguished. In sixteenth-century England there was a strong connection between the Inns and the burgeoning theatre. In 1561 the first blank-verse tragedy, *Gorboduc*, was put on in Inner Temple Hall, and later new plays were often tried out in the Inns: *Twelfth Night* for example had its first night in Middle Temple Hall in 1602. Both these Inns preserve the theatrical tradition by summoning their students to 'eat their dinners' (as the phrase goes) with a flourish, the Middle Temple with a hunting horn, the Inner Temple with a silver-mounted ram's horn.

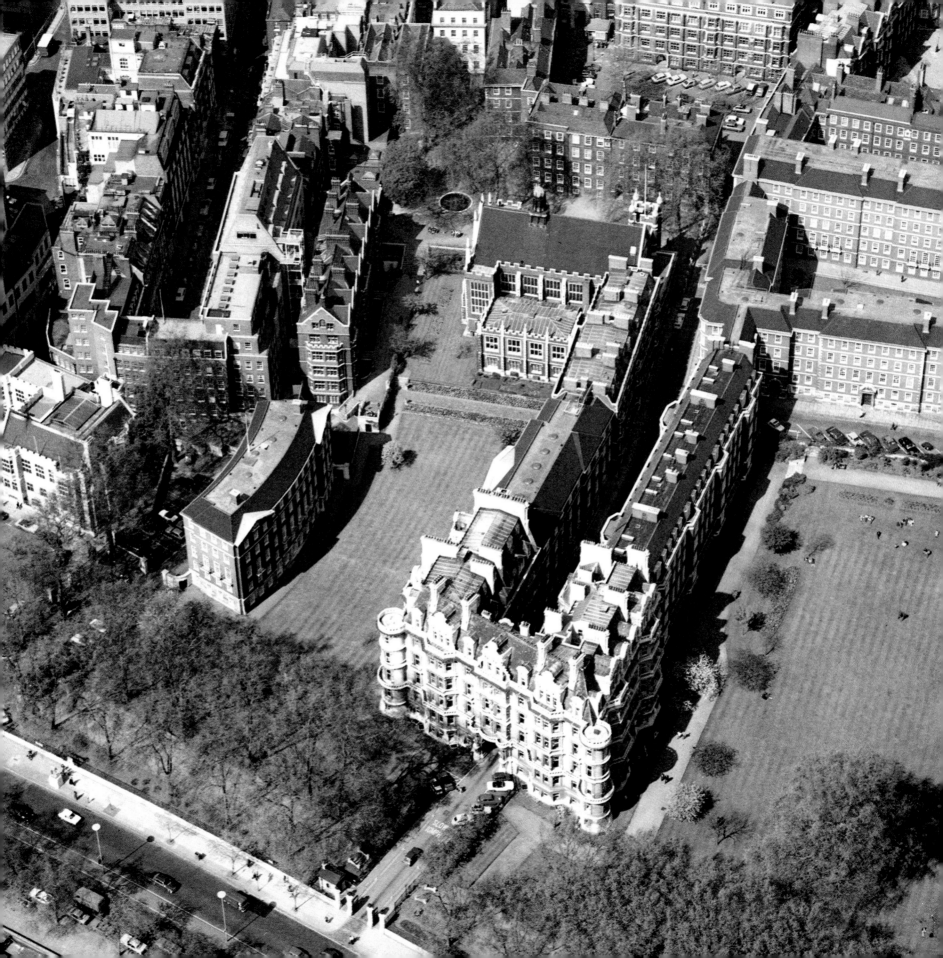

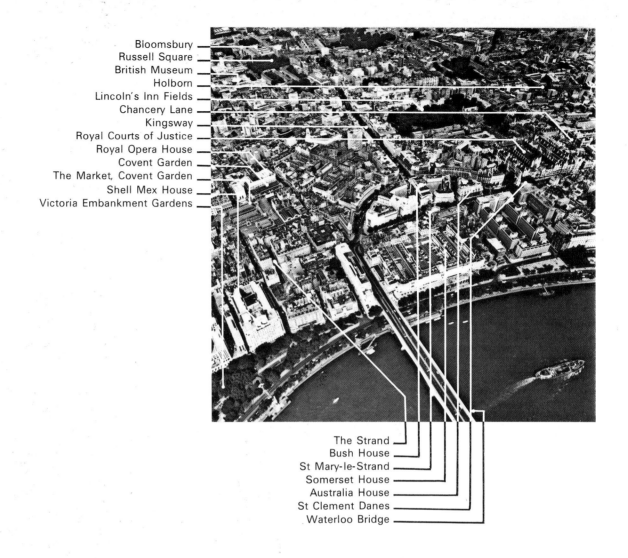

Bloomsbury
Russell Square
British Museum
Holborn
Lincoln's Inn Fields
Chancery Lane
Kingsway
Royal Courts of Justice
Royal Opera House
Covent Garden
The Market, Covent Garden
Shell Mex House
Victoria Embankment Gardens

The Strand
Bush House
St Mary-le-Strand
Somerset House
Australia House
St Clement Danes
Waterloo Bridge

THE ALDWYCH

This chunk of west-central London by the river is really an annexe to Whitehall, with architecture of governmental flavour. It was originally occupied by two of the great riverine mansions built by nobles between the Temple and Westminster: Arundel House on the right, Somerset House on the left. Protector Somerset started to build a palace here in the late 1540s but it was never finished, since in 1552 he had his head chopped off. Thereafter it reverted to the Crown. In the 1770s it was decided to pull it down and Sir William Chambers was asked to design a building suitable for various government offices. He produced an enormous Palladian front, 600 feet long, resting on a rusticated terrace 50 feet above the Embankment, whose Piranesian central arch was once the water-gate entrance. It is one of only four major buildings (the others are Parliament, Greenwich and County Hall) worthy of London's majestic river, and is beautifully enhanced by Sir Giles Gilbert Scott's Waterloo Bridge (1934), one of the handsomest on the Thames. Across the Strand, on the other side of James Gibbs's delightful St Mary-le-Strand (1714), is a complementary group of official buildings put up in Edwardian times and later, also in Palladian, but with the unmistakable whiff of the late-imperial age of Elgar, Kipling and Lutyens. Actually, Lutyens had nothing to do with them. But India House (1928) is by his colleague Sir Herbert Baker, and Marshall Mackenzie's Australia House (1912), at the eastern end, is very Crown Imperial. The middle group, Bush House (1925), is by an American firm, Helmle & Corbett, though you wouldn't think it, so well has the mood of twilit grandeur been caught. By contrast, the 1970s block on the site of old Arundel House is in the anonymous International Style and could be anywhere, from Phnom Penh to Kansas City.

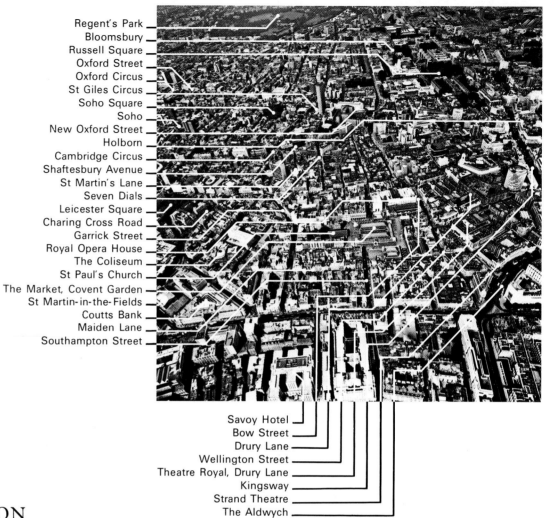

Regent's Park —
Bloomsbury —
Russell Square —
Oxford Street —
Oxford Circus —
St Giles Circus —
Soho Square —
Soho —
New Oxford Street —
Holborn —
Cambridge Circus —
Shaftesbury Avenue —
St Martin's Lane —
Seven Dials —
Leicester Square —
Charing Cross Road —
Garrick Street —
Royal Opera House —
The Coliseum —
St Paul's Church —
The Market, Covent Garden —
St Martin-in-the-Fields —
Coutts Bank —
Maiden Lane —
Southampton Street —

Savoy Hotel —
Bow Street —
Drury Lane —
Wellington Street —
Theatre Royal, Drury Lane —
Kingsway —
Strand Theatre —
The Aldwych —

THEATREGOERS' LONDON

The centre of the picture is Covent Garden, where in 1631 the fourth Earl of Bedford, whose family had grabbed the garden from the Westminster monks, and Inigo Jones planned the Italian-style piazza which marked the real beginning of the West End. Little remains of the original arcades, and even the fruit and vegetable market (forming the background to the opening of Shaw's *Pygmalion*, alias *My Fair Lady*) has gone; Charles Fowler's pretty market building of 1825 has been turned into a *souk* of smart shops, stalls and coffee shops, the centre of what is now London's liveliest district. But Inigo Jones's St Paul's, built at the same time as the original piazza, is still there with its stupendous portico. It is the church of the theatrical profession and, indeed, this is theatregoers' London. At the north-east corner is E.M. Barry's Royal Opera House (1857). Two streets away to the east is the Theatre Royal, Drury Lane. Running diagonally west from the back of St Paul's churchyard is Garrick Street with the Garrick Club, jointly dominated by actors and lawyers. Nearby is the Ivy, London's most

famous theatrical restaurant, in Ivy Lane, and in St Martin's Lane the English National Opera Company performs at London's second opera house, the Coliseum. Also on St Martin's Lane are two famous theatres, the Albany and the Duke of York's, while the Garrick and Wyndham's are on Charing Cross Road. The most northerly of the theatres are at Seven Dials and St Giles Circus. Then, going down Shaftesbury Avenue westwards, there is the Palace on Cambridge Circus, and a string of famous stages between there and Piccadilly Circus. In the bottom right-hand corner of our picture are the Strand and Aldwych theatres at either end of the north-east segment of the Aldwych. In the Strand itself, the Savoy nestles in the bosom of the Savoy Hotel, while on the north side are the Vaudeville and the Adelphi. Not to be missed on the Strand is the triangle of Coutts Bank, with its twin pepperpot domes by Nash (1830) and a chunk of modern glasswork in the middle.

Park Crescent
Marylebone
Hyde Park
Oxford Street
Oxford Circus
Regent Street
Soho
Green Park
Lower Regent Street
St James's
Leicester Square
Waterloo Place

Duke of York's Steps
Charing Cross Station
Whitehall Place
Whitehall Court

Portland Place
Wardour Street
Dean Street
Frith Street
Greek Street
Soho Square
Regent's Park

CHARING CROSS

On 2 April 1775, dining with Dr Johnson, Boswell 'talked of the cheerfulness of Fleet-street, owing to the constant quick procession of people we perceive passing through it.' Dr Johnson: 'Why, Sir, Fleet Street has a very animated appearance. But I think the full tide of human existence is at Charing Cross.' Charing Cross itself has nothing to do with the 1863 railway station, built by John Hawkshaw on the site of the old Hungerford Market; it was the last of the crosses set up by Edward I to mark the places where the body of his beloved wife Eleanor had rested on its way to her Westminster tomb. Here is the 'hub of empire', as Kipling put it. To the left of Charing Cross is Whitehall Place, with the striking block known as Whitehall Court (1884) and, just off the picture, Waterhouse's National Liberal Club (1885), architecturally the most interesting club in London. Then, like spokes in the wheel, are Whitehall and The Mall. From

there we can see the daring of Nash's great scheme to carve a triumphal way through west London: up the Duke of York's steps, between the two wings of Carlton House Terrace, between the Athenaeum and the Institute of Directors, up Lower Regent Street and then, at Piccadilly Circus, wheeling a quarter-turn left (the Quadrant) to go up Regent's Street, across Oxford Circus, then through Portland Place to debouch in Park Crescent at the entrance to Regent's Park. What a noble enterprise lost! Centre-right of the picture is the green of Leicester Square; beyond it is Gerrard Street, the new Chinese quarter, and, beyond that and Shaftesbury Avenue, the four parallel main streets of Soho: Wardour Street (the film quarter), Dean, Frith and Greek Streets, with the green blob of Soho Square at the end of the last two. Beyond that again, the long line of Oxford Street stretches westwards.

Sussex Place
National Portrait Gallery
National Gallery
Nelson's Column
Admiralty Arch

Whitehall
Canada House (ex Royal College of Physicians)
Northumberland Avenue

TRAFALGAR SQUARE

At the end of the eighteenth century the open space west of Charing Cross was really nothing more than the Royal Mews (now on the south side of Buckingham Palace) and the entrance to St James's Park. It was Nash's idea in 1812 to turn it into a victory square to mark Britain's triumphs in the wars against Napoleon. The idea took shape after Robert Smirke put up the classical Royal College of Physicians (now Canada House) in 1825 on the west side of the space and William Wilkins the National Gallery (1832) on the north side. This was a classical building too, as of course was James Gibbs's superb St Martin-in-the-Fields (1722) in the top right-hand corner. To build a victory column was itself a classical idea, derived from Traja's Column in Rome, which the French had already imitated in the Place Vendôme in Paris. The square was christened in 1830 but not until eight years later was a committee set up to devise a Nelson Memorial. In 1840 William Railton was commissioned to design it. The column, then by far the highest of its kind in the world, was a notable

engineering achievement, being set up in a single day, 3 November 1843, between 6.46 and 11.20 a.m., by non-union labour (there was a masons' strike). The lions caused great trouble. After two disastrous failures by professional sculptors, the job was handed to the animal painter, Sir Edwin Landseer, who pulled it off. Barry's fountains did not work, producing merely what was termed 'the overflow from a beer bottle', and had to be remodelled by Lutyens in the 1930s, as part of his scheme to commemorate the First World War Admirals Beatty and Jellicoe. The other hero of the square is General Gordon. Despite its martial tone, the square is the favourite of anti-establishment protesters. The first demonstration, in March 1848, was against raising income tax. 'Black Monday' followed in February 1886, 'Bloody Sunday' in November the next year. The square has since been used by Fascists, Communists, nuclear disarmers and New Year's Eve revellers to make their various points.

NOTE ON SOURCES

The London volumes in the Penguin *Buildings of England* series (founding editor Nikolaus Pevsner) have been my most trusted sources in compiling the captions of this book; I have also used the *Survey of London*, the *Victoria County Histories* and numerous guides. Specialist studies I have found useful include Peter Marsden, *Roman London* (1980); R. Merrifield, *The Archaeology of London* (1975); W.R. Dalzell, *The Shell Guide to the History of London* (1981); Kevin McDonnell, *Medieval London Suburbs* (1978); Peter Jackson, *London Bridge* (1971); John Stow, *A Survey of London*, ed. C.L. Kingsford (2 vols, Oxford 1908); Eric de Maré, *Wren's London* (1975); George Rudé, *Hanoverian London, 1714–1808* (1971); Stella Margetson, *Regency London* (1971); John Betjeman, *Victorian and Edwardian London* (1969); Alastair Service, *London 1900* (1979); Simon Jenkins, *Landlords to London: the Story of a Capital and its Growth* (1975); Gavin Weightman and Steve Humphries, *The Making of Modern London* (1983); Guy R. Williams, *London in the Country: the Growth of Suburbia* (1975); Arthur Mee, *London North of the Thames* (1972 ed.); Simon Jenkins, *The Companion Guide to Outer London* (1981); Charles Harris, *Islington* (1974); Reginald Colby, *Mayfair: a Town within London* (1966); Geoffrey Evans, *Kensington* (1975); D. Marshall, *Dr Johnson's London* (1968).

Aerofilms Ltd have been photographing Britain from the air since 1919, when F.L. Wills and Claude Graham White, the company's founders, took an open seater bi-plane up over Hendon, north London, and photographed the area. Since then over three-quarters of a million aerial photographs have been added to Aerofilms archives, forming a unique and comprehensive collection.

INDEX

Adam, James, 110
Adam, Robert, 50, 110
Adelphi Theatre, 164
Admiralty, 50
Admiralty House, 50
Agar Grove housing estate, 122
The Albany, 92
Albert, Prince, 86
Albemarle Street, 92
Albert Bridge, 82
Albert Gate, 90
Albert Hall *see* Royal Albert Hall
Albert Memorial, 86, 88
Albery Theatre, 164
Aldersgate, 14, 138
Aldersgate Street, 138
Aldgate, 14
Aldgate East tube station, 136
Aldwych, 162, 164
Aldwych Theatre, 164
Alexandra Gate, 90
Alfred, King, 5
All Hallows, Barking, 142
All Saints, Camden Town, 122
All Saints, Ennismore Gardens, 86
All Souls, Langham Place, 110
Amery, Julian, 70
Anchor Inn, Bankside, 36
Angel Inn, 32
Anglo-Saxon London, 5, 12, 14
Anne, Queen, 62, 84
Anne Boleyn, 16, 62
Anne of Denmark, Queen, 26
Apothecaries' Hall, 148
Apsley House, 92
Archbishop's House, Westminster, 56
Archer, Thomas, 56, 80
Argyle House, King's Road, 82
aristocratic estates, 6, 7–8, 10, 64
Arlington, Earl of, 66
Armoury House, 134
Army Museum, Tite Street, 82
Arts and Crafts style, 70
Arundel House, 6, 46, 162
Asquith, Herbert Henry, Earl of Oxford
    and, 38
Athenaeum, 60

Attlee, Clement, 18
Aubrey, John, 136
Audley, Hugh, 64
Audley Street, 104
Austen, Jane, 128
Australia House, 162
Avery Row, 92

Babington, Anthony, 112
Baker, Sir Herbert, 56, 102, 140, 162
Baker Street, 106
Baldwin, Stanley, 102
Bank of England, 5, 140, 144
Bankside, 36
Bankside Power Station, 36
Banqueting House, Whitehall, 46, 50
Barbican, 134, 138, 142, 148
Barking, 24
Barlow, W.H., 126
Barnard's Inn, 158
Barnsbury, 126
Barry, Sir Charles, 52, 60, 126, 168
Barry, E.M., 164
Basildon New Town, 76
Bath House, Serpentine, 90
Battersea Bridge, 82
Battersea Park, 82, 104
Battersea Power Station, 74, 80
'Battle of Cable Street' (1926), 20
Baynard's Castle, 38
Bayswater, 96, 156
Bazalgette, Sir Joseph, 158
BBC, 110
Bear Gardens, Bear Lane, 36
Beaufort Gardens, 86
Beaufort Street, 82
Bedford, Russells, Earl of, 6, 7, 164
Bedford College, 116
Bedford Square, 7, 8
Bedlam (Royal Bethlehem Hospital), 42
Beech Street, 138
Belfast, HMS, 14
Belgrave Square, 7, 68
Belgravia, 7, 10, 64, 68, 70, 76, 78
Belsize Park, 116, 120
Bentham, Jeremy, 72
Bentley, J.F., 58

Berkeley estate, 7, 92
Berkeley Hotel, 68
Berkeley Square, 7, 92, 104
Berkeley Street, 104
Bermondsey, 32
Bermondsey Street, 32
Bethnal Green Gasworks, 132
Bickenhall Mansions, 106
Big Ben, 52
Billingsgate fish market, 14
Birdcage Walk, 56
Bishopsgate, 8, 14, 144, 146
Blackfriars, 38, 40
Blackfriars Bridge, 36, 38, 142
Blackfriars Lane, 148
Blackfriars Station, 38
Black Lion Yard, 136
Black Prince Road, 42
Blackwall, 22, 24
Blenheim Crescent, 98
Blomfield, Arthur, 86
Bloomsbury, 7, 64, 108, 128
Bloomsbury Group, 128
Blore, Edward, 66
Bond Street, 64, 104
Boodles Club, 60
Boothby, Lord, 70
Borough High Street, 34
Boswell, James, 166
Bouverie Street, 154
Bracknell Gardens, 120
Bradlaugh, Charles, 112
Bricklayers Arms Goods Station, 32
Bridewell Palace, 38, 66
British Museum, 108, 130
    King's Library, 66, 130
    Reading Room, 130
British Rail HQ, 124
British Steel Corporation, 68
British Telecom Tower (Post Office
    Tower), 108
Broacasting House, Portland Place, 108,
    110
Broad Street, 8
Broad Walk, Regent's Park, 124
Brompton, 86
Brompton Oratory, 86

Brompton Road, 86
Brook House, Park Lane, 92
Brook Street, 104
Brooks's Club, 60
Brunswick Square, 128
Bruton Street, 92
Brydon, J.M., 50
Buckingham, Duke of, 66
Buckingham Palace, 66, 70, 90, 104
    Gardens, 6, 48, 66
Buckingham Palace Road, 64
Bucklersbury House, 38
Bunhill Fields, 132
Burbage, James, 134
Burbage, Richard, 36
Burges, William, 102
Burghley, William Cecil, Lord, 44
Burlington House (Royal Academy), 92
Burne-Jones, Sir Edward, 70
Burton, Decimus, 60, 116, 118
Bush House, 162
Butler, Lord ('Rab'), 70
Byron, Lord, 102
Byron Villas, Hampstead, 120

Cabinet Offices, 50
Cadogan estate, 7, 68
Cadogan Places, 68
Cadogan Square, 7, 68, 86
Caledonian Road, 126
Camberwell, 30
Cambridge Circus, 164
Cambridge Heath Road, 136
Cambridge Square, 96
Camden Street, 122
Camden Town, 108, 116, 122
Cannon Street, 140
Cannon Street Station, 12, 34, 140
Canvey Island, 76
Capital Radio, 108
Cardigan, Earl of, 44
Carey Street, 158
Carlton Club, 60
Carlton House Terrace, 8, 60, 124, 166
Carlton Tower Hotel, 68
Carlyle, Thomas, 82
Caroline, Queen, 62

Casement, Sir Roger, 16
Catherine Howard, 16
Catherine of Aragon, 38
Cavendish Square, 7, 104
Cecil family, 44
Central Criminal Court (Old Bailey), 148
Central Electricity Generating Board, 80
Central Land Registry, 158
Central Hall, Westminster, 56
Centre Point, 108, 146, 156
Chambers, Sir William, 162
Chamber's Cold Storage Wharf, 32
Chancery Lane, 156, 158
Change Alley, 144
Channon, Sir Henry ('Chips'), 70
Charing Cross, 10, 48, 78, 104, 166, 168
Charing Cross Road, 108, 164
Charing Cross Station, 34, 40, 166
Charles I, King, 46, 48, 62, 90
Charles II, King, 26, 32, 46, 48, 62, 82
Charles Street, 92
Charlotte Street, 128
Charterhouse, 138
Chaucer, Geoffrey, 34
Cheapside, 12, 140, 156
Chelsea, 7, 10, 48, 78, 82, 104
Chelsea Barracks, 78
Chelsea Bridge, 74, 76, 78
Chelsea Royal Hospital, 7, 78, 82
Chester Square, 7, 64, 70
Cheyne Row, 82
Cheyne Walk, 82
Chichester, Sir Francis, 26
Chiltern Court, Marylebone, 106
Christ Church, Spitalfields, 18
Church House, Westminster, 56
Churchill, Winston, 14, 102
    wartime bunker of, 50
Churchill Gardens Estate, 74, 80
Citadel, Whitehall, 50
City of London, 5, 6, 7, 8, 10, 12, 46, 124,
    140, 142, 144, 146, 148
City of London School, 38
City Road, 132, 134
City University, 132
Clapham, 64, 82
Claridges Hotel, 104
Claverton Street, 74
Clerkenwell, 128, 132
Clerkenwell Road, 132
Cleveland Street, 108
Clink prison, Southwark, 34
Clock Tower Estate, Camden Town, 122
Clore, Charles, 118

clubs, 60, 92, 166
Cobb Street, 136
Cockerell, C.R., 102
Cockerell, S.P., 50
Coliseum, 164
College of Arms, 38
Commercial Road, 136
Connaught Hotel, 104
Copenhagen Fields, 152
Coram's Fields, 128
Cornhill, 12, 144
Cornmarket Street, 140
Costain, Sir Richard, 74
Cotton, Jack, 118
County Fire Office, 94
County Hall, 40, 46
Coutts' Bank, Strand, 164
Covent Garden, 6, 7, 164
    Market, 164
    Royal Opera House, 164
Covent Garden Square, 6, 60
Crew House, Curzon Street, 92
Cringle Dock, 76
Cripplegate, 14
Criterion Theatre, 94
Cromwell, Thomas, 62
Crumden, J., 60
Cubitt, Lewis and Joseph, 126
Cubitt, Thomas, 64, 70, 74, 76
Cumberland, Duke of, 62
Cumberland Terrace, 116
Cundy, Thomas, 64, 78
Cundy III, Thomas, 64, 70
Curtain Theatre, 134
Curzon Street, 92
Customs House, 14, 142
Cutlers' Hall, 148
Cutty Sark, 26

Dance the Elder, George, 132, 140
Dance the Younger, George, 134, 144,
    156
Davies, Mary, 7, 64, 92
Davies Street, 104
Davy, Sir Humphry, 118
Dean Street, 166
Dean's Yard, 56
Defence, Ministry of, 46, 50
Deptford, 30
Derby House, 38
Devonshire Club, 60
Devonshire House, 92
Dickens, Charles 6, 8, 9, 34, 38, 122, 158
Disraeli, Benjamin, 92

dissolution of religious houses, 6, 48, 64
'Division Bell Area', 56
Dolphin Square, 74
Dover House, 50
Dorchester Hotel, 92
Dorset House, Baker Street, 106
Dowbiggin, Lancelot, 30
Downing Street, 50
Drury Lane Theatre Royal, 164
Dudley House, 92
Duke of York's Barracks, King's Road,
    82
Duke of York's Steps, 166
Duke of York's Theatre, 164
Dutch Church, Old Broad Street, 144

Eastcheap, 12, 140, 142
East End of London, 8, 18, 20, 22, 24,
    124, 136
East Ham, 24
Eaton Place, 68
Eaton Square, 7, 64, 68, 70
Ebury Bridge, 78
Ebury, Manor of, 7
Edgware Road, 96, 106, 112
Edward I, King, 16, 152, 164
Edward III, King, 42
Edward V, King, 16
Edward VI, King, 38
Edward the Black Prince, 42
Edward the Confessor, 5, 52, 54
Egerton Gardens, 86
Egerton Terrace, 86
Elephant and Castle, 8, 40, 42
Elgin Crescent, 98
Eliot, George, 112
Elizabeth I, Queen, 16, 26, 62, 84, 112,
    138
Elizabeth Street, 64
'El Vino's', Fleet Street, 154
English Opera Company, 164
Ennismore Gardens, 86
Eros fountain, Piccadilly, 94
Essex House, 46
Eton College, 102
Euston, 8, 10, 124
Euston Centre, 124, 128
Euston House, 108
Euston Road, 108, 124, 128
Euston Station, 122, 124
Evelyn, John, 26, 82

Faraday Building, 38
Farm Street, 92

Farringdon Road, 154
Fenchurch Street, 140, 144
Fenchurch Street Station, 8, 14, 142
Ferrey, Benjamin, 56
Fetter Lane, 154
Finchley Road, 112
Finsbury Circus, 134, 142, 144
Finsbury Square, 134
'Fitzrovia', 128
Fitzroy Square, 128
Flask Walk, 120
Fleet, river, 12
Fleet Street, 6, 46, 148, 154, 158, 166
Fordham Street, 136
Foreign and Commonwealth Office, 50
Forster, E.M., 128
Founders Arms pub, 38
Fowke, Captain, 86
Fowler, Charles, 164
Freemasons' Hall, 156
French Huguenots, 134
Friends' House, Euston Road, 124
Frith Street, 166
Frognal, Hampstead, 120
Fry, Roger, 128
Fulham, 82

Galsworthy, John, 120
Gardiner, Bishop, 34
Garrick Club, 164
Garrick Street, 164
Garrick Theatre, 164
General Accident offices, 68
General Strike (1926), 20
Geological Museum, 86
George III, King, 62, 66, 90
George IV, King (formerly Prince
    Regent), 8, 10, 60, 66, 94, 130
George V, King, 60, 62, 66
George Inn, Southwark, 34
Geraldine Mary Harmsworth Park, 42
German Blitz (1940–5), 8, 14, 18, 52, 136,
    148
Gerrard Street, 166
Gibbs, James, 162, 168
Gilbert, Alfred, 94
Gipsy Moth IV, 26
Globe Insurance, 144
Globe Theatre, 36
Gloucester, Humphrey, Duke of, 26
Gloucester Gate, 116
Goldsmiths' Hall, 148
Gording, Lord, 66
Gordon Square, 128

Goswell Road, 132
Gough House, 82
Gould, James, 144
Gower Street, 108, 128
Gracechurch Street, 144
Grant, Duncan, 128
Gray, Thomas, 130
Gray's Inn, 158
Gray's Inn gardens, 156
Gray's Inn Road, 126, 128, 154, 156
Great Central Hotel, Marylebone, 106
Great Fire of London (1666), 6–7, 14, 150
Great Ormond Street, 128
Great Tower Street, 142
Greek Street, 166
Green Park, 6, 48, 60, 104
Greenwich, 26
    Cutty Sark, 26
    Gipsy Moth IV, 26
    Hospital, 7, 26
    National Maritime Museum (Queen's House), 26
    Observatory, 26
    Royal Naval College, 26
Gresham, Sir Thomas, 140
Gresham House, 146
Gresham Street, 148
Gribble, Herbert, 86
Gronow, Captain, 90
Grosvenor, Sir Richard, 7, 64, 92
Grosvenor estates, 7, 64, 68, 70, 74, 92
Grosvenor Hotel, 78, 92
Grosvenor Place, 64, 68
Grosvenor Square, 7, 92, 104
Grosvenor Street, 92
Grove End Road, 112
Grove House, Regent's Park, 116
Grove Lodge, Well Walk, 120
Gundulf, Bishop of Rochester, 16
Gunthorpe Street, 136
Guy's Hospital, 34
Gwydyr House, 50

Haggerston, 132
Haileybury mission, 18
Hakewell, Henry, 64
Halliday, J. and Agate, 80
Hammersmith, 82
Hampstead, 112, 120
Hampstead Heath, 120
Hampstead Road, 108
Hampton Court Palace, 7, 46, 84
Hanover Square, 7

Hans Place, 86
Hardwick, Thomas, 112, 132
Harrods, 86
Harrow School, 102
Hatton Garden, 6
Haverstock Hill, 116
Hawksmoor, Nicholas, 7, 18, 24, 26, 54, 144
Hawshaw, John, 166
Haymarket, 60
Hayward Gallery, 40
Heath, Edward, 92
Helmle & Corbett, 162
Henry III, King, 16, 52, 54
Henry VI, King, 16
Henry VII, King, 26
Henry VIII, King, 6, 7, 10, 16, 26, 38, 44, 46, 48, 60, 62, 64, 66, 84, 90, 134, 138
Henslowe, Philip, 36
Hess, Rudolf, 16
Heywood, William, 154
Highbury, 64
High Holborn, 154, 156
Hill Street, 92
Hilton Hotel, 104, 108, 146, 156
Hippodrome racecourse, 98
Hobbs, Jack, 42
Hogarth, William, 12
Holborn, 7, 108, 154, 156
Holborn Circus, 154
Holborn Viaduct, 154
Holford, Lord, 12, 148
Holland, Henry, 50, 60, 92
Holland Park, 96, 98
Holland Park Road, 98
The Holme, Regent's Park, 116
Holy Trinity, Brompton Road, 86
Holy Trinity, Marylebone Road, 124
Holy Trinity, Sloane Street, 70
Home Office, 50, 56
Honourable Artillery Company, 134
Horseferry Road, 56
Horse Guards, 50
Horse Guards Parade, 46, 50
Houses of Parliament, 9, 46, 52, 56, 126
Hungerford Railway Bridge, 40, 104
Howland Street, 108
Hunt, Leigh, 120
Huxley, Aldous, 120
Huxley, Dr Julian, 118
Huxley, Thomas, 112
Hyde Park, 6, 7, 48, 68, 86, 90, 96, 106, 116, 156

Hyde Park Corner, 48, 64, 92
Hyde Park Barracks, 68
Hyde Park Hotel, 68

Imperial Chemical Industries, 72
Imperial College of Science and Technology, 86
Imperial War Museum, 42
India House, 162
Inner Temple, 158, 160
Inner Temple Hall, 160
Inns of Court, 158, 160
Institute of Directors, 60, 166
International Press Building, 154
Inwood, William and Charles, 122, 124
Ironmongers' Hall, 148
Islamic Cultural Centre, 112
Isle of Dogs, 24
Islington, 124, 126, 132
Italian Garden, Hyde Park, 90
'Ivy', theatrical restaurant, 164

Jack the Ripper, 136
Jacob's Street, 32
James I, King, 16, 26, 48, 62, 66, 84, 138
James II, King, 62
James Edward Stuart, Old Pretender, 62
Jenkins, Simon, 100
Jermyn Street, 60
Jewish Burial Ground, 22
Jewish East End, 20, 22
John of Gaunt, 6, 46
Johnson, Dr Samuel, 26, 36, 62, 120, 160, 166
Jones, Sir Horace, 14, 152
Jones, Inigo, 6, 46, 156, 164
Jonson, Ben, 34
'Journalists' London', 154

Keats, John, 120
Kennington, 42, 72
Kennington Lane, 42
Kensington, 8, 10
    'Academic', 86, 88
Kensington Gardens, 6, 90, 96
Kensington Gore, 86
Kensington Palace, 48, 66, 86
Kent, William, 50
Keynes, J.M., 128
Kilburn, 112
King's Bench prison, Southwark, 34
King's Bench Walk, 160
King's Cross Goods Depot, 122
King's Cross Station, 8, 122, 124, 126, 128

King's Reach development, 36
King's Road, 68, 70, 82
King's Square, 132
Kingsland Road, 132
Knightsbridge, 68
Knott, Ralph, 40
Knowles, J.T., 78

Ladbroke estate, 98
Ladbroke Gardens, 98
Ladbroke Grove, 98
Ladbroke Square Gardens, 98
Lambeth, 42
Lambeth Bridge, 72
Lambeth Palace, 6, 56
    Park, 42
Lancaster House, 60
Landseer, Sir Edwin, 112, 168
Langham Hotel, 110
Langham Place, 110
Lansdowne Crescent, 98
Lansdowne House, 92
Lansdowne Passage, 92
Lansdowne Road, 98
Lasdun, Denys, 124
Law Courts, 9, 126, 148
Lawrence, D.H., 120
Law Society, 158
'Lawyers' London', 158, 160
Le Nôtre, 84
Lea, river, 24
Leadenhall Street, 142
Leathermarket, 32
Leathermarket Street, 32
Lees, Robert, 136
Leicester Square, 166
Lennox Gardens, 86
Lever Street, 132
Lewis, James, 42
Lilestone, Manor of, 7
Limehouse, 24
Lincoln's Inn, 158
Lincoln's Inn Fields, 6, 60, 156, 158
Lisson Green Estate, 112
Liverpool Street Station, 8, 14, 134, 136, 142, 144
Liverpool Victoria Friendly Society, 156
Lloyds Computer Centre, 36
Lombard Street, 12, 140, 144
London, George, 84
London Bridge, 7, 8, 10, 12, 38, 140, 144
London Bridge Station, 30
London Fields, 132
London Museum, Barbican, 134, 148

London Park Tower Hotel, 68
London Pavilion, 94
London School of Economics, 156
London Symphony Orchestra, 134
London Wall, 5, 134
London Weekend Television tower, 36
Londonderry House, Park Lane, 8, 92
Long Water, Hyde Park, 90
Lord's Cricket Ground (MCC), 44, 112, 114
Lower Regent Street, 94, 166
Lower Thames Street, 142
Ludgate, 14
Ludgate Circus, 148
Ludgate Hill, 148, 154
Lupus Street, 74
Lutyens, Sir Edwin, 72, 134, 154, 162, 168

Macaulay, Lord, 92
Mackenzie, Marshall, 162
Madame Tussaud's, 106
Maida Vale, 112
The Mall, 60, 66, 110, 166
Manchester Square, 104
Manning, Cardinal, 58
Mansfield, Katherine, 120
Mansion House, 5, 140
Marble Arch, 66, 90
Marlborough Gate, 90
Marlborough House, 60
Marshalsea Prison, 34, 122
Marsham Street, 56
Marx, Karl, 130
Mary I, Queen ('Bloody Mary'), 34, 62, 152
Mary II of Orange, Queen, 84
Mary of Modena, Queen, 62
Mary Queen of Scots, 138
Marylebone, 7, 104, 106, 108, 112
Marylebone Lane, 104
Marylebone Road, 106, 124
Marylebone Station, 106, 112, 124
Masefield, John, 120
Master of the Rolls, 158
Mayfair, 7, 64, 68, 92, 104, 108
Melbourne House, 92
Merchant Taylors' School, 138
Mermaid Theatre, 38
Middle Temple, 158, 160
Middle Temple Lane, 160
Mile End Road, 20, 22, 136
Millbank, 64, 72
Millbank Estate, 72

Mill Wall, 24
Mincing Lane, 144
Minories, 142
Montague House, 130
Montague Square, 7
Moore, G.E., 128
Moorfield Eye Hospital, 134
Moorfields, 134
Moorgate in the Wall, 134
Moorgate, 134
More, Sir Thomas, 7, 16, 82
Morocco Street, 32
Mortimer Crescent, 120
Mosley, Oswald, 20
Mount Street, 92, 104
Mulberry Garden, Buckingham Palace, 66
Murray, John, publishers, 92
Murray, Middleton, 120
Mylne, Robert, 38, 42

Nash, John, 8, 10, 60, 66, 94, 96, 110, 116, 118, 124, 164, 166, 168
National Farmers Union, 68
National Film Theatre, 40
National Gallery, 168
National Liberal Club, 166
National Theatre, 40
Natural History Museum, 9, 86, 88
NatWest Tower, 142, 144, 146
Naval and Military Club, 92
Nelson's Column, 168
New Bond Street, 104
New Bridge Street, 38
Newby, Frank, 118
Newcastle, Duke of, 104
New Covent Garden Market, 74
    see also Covent Garden
Newgate, 14, 148
    'Shambles', 152
Newgate Street, 148, 154, 156
New North Road, 132
New Oxford Street, 108, 156
New Road, Whitechapel, 136
New Scotland Yard, 56
newspaper offices see 'Journalists' London'
Nine Elms Lane, 74
Norfolk, fourth Duke of, 138
Norman London, 5, 14, 16
Northampton Square, 132
North Audley Street, 104
North Barbican or Golden Lane Estate, 138
North Road, 122

Notting Hill, 96, 98
Notting Hill Gate, 48, 96

Old Bailey, 148
Old Broad Street, 144, 146
Old St Pancras Church, 122
Old St Paul's, 150
Old Street, 132
Old Tabard Inn, Southwark, 34
Old Treasury, Whitehall, 50
Old Vic Theatre, 36
Open Air Theatre, Regent's Park, 116
Ordish, R.M., 126
Orwell, George, 120
Oval (Surrey Cricket Club), 42, 72
Ovington Square, 86
Oxford, Harleys, Earls of, 7
Oxford and Cambridge Club, 60
Oxford Circus, 94, 104, 108, 166
Oxford Square, 96
Oxford Street, 7, 92, 104, 156, 166
Oxo Warehouse tower, 36

Paddington, 8, 10, 106
Paddington Basin, 96
Paddington Station, 96, 124
Page Street council flats, 72
Palace Theatre, 164
Pall Mall, 60
Palmerston, Lord, 50, 92, 102, 126
Panizzi, Anthony, 130
Park Crescent, 110, 124, 166
Park Lane, 8, 90, 92, 104
Park Road, 112
Park Square Gardens, 124
Park Street, Southwark, 36
Park Streets East and West, Regent's Park, 124
Parliament Hill, 120
Parliament Square, 46
Paternoster Square, 148
Pearl Assurance building, 156
Peckham, 30
Peel, Sir Robert, 102
Pentonville, 122
Pentonville Road, 126
People's Palace, 22
Pepys, Samuel, 28
Peter Hills School, 30
Pevsner, Nikolaus, 110, 114
Piccadilly, 60, 92, 104, 108
Piccadilly Circus, 94, 104, 164, 166
Pimlico, 10, 74, 78, 104
Pimlico refuse barges, 76

Pimlico Road, 78
Pitsea Marshes, 76
Plasterers' Hall, 148
Pont Street, 68, 86
'Pont Street Dutch' style, 86
Poplar, 8, 24
Portland, Dukes of, 7, 104, 116
Portland Place, 94, 108, 110, 124
Portland stone, 7, 40, 148
Portman estates, 7
Poynter, Ambrose, 116
Praed, William, 96
Praed Street, 96
Price, Cedric, 118
Primrose Hill, 116
Prince Albert Road, 124
Prince Regent see George IV
Printing House Square, 154
Prudential Building, 9, 156
Public Order Act (1936), 20
Pudding Lane, 6
Putney, 82
Putney Bridge, 38

Quadrant, Piccadilly Circus, 94, 166
Queen Elizabeth Hall, 40
Queen Mary College, 22
Queen Victoria Street, 38

Raffles, Sir Stamford, 118
Ranelagh Gardens, 78
Ratcliff, 22
Red Lion Square, 156
Reform Club, 60
Regent Street, 8, 92, 94, 104, 108, 110, 166
Regent's Canal, 24, 96, 112, 116, 122, 126, 132
Regent's Canal Dock, 24, 96
Regent's Park, 7, 8, 94, 96, 106, 110, 112, 116, 124, 128, 166
    inner and outer circles, 10, 116
    Open Air Theatre, 116
    Zoological Gardens, 116, 118
Rennie, George, 90
Rennie, John, 12
Reuters and Press Association headquarters, 154
Richard II, King, 52, 152
Ripley, Thomas, 50
Ritz Hotel, 104
Roman London, 5, 10, 12, 14, 34, 38, 140
Rose Theatre, 36

Rossetti, Dante Gabriel, 82
Rotherhithe, 8, 24, 30
Rotten Row, 90
Round Pond, 86, 96
Royal Academy of Arts, 92
Royal Albert Hall, 86, 88
Royal Automobile Club, 60
Royal College of Music, 86
Royal College of Physicians, 124, 168
Royal College of Surgeons, 156
Royal College Street, 122
Royal Courts of Justice, 5, 158
Royal Exchange, 140
Royal Festival Hall, 40
Royal Mews, 168
Royal Mint, 18
Royal Opera House see Covent Garden
Royal Shakespeare Company, 134
Royal Veterinary College, 122
Royal Watermen, 66
Russell Square, 128

St Albans, Henry Jermyn, Lord, 6, 60
St Andrew, Holborn, 154
St Andrew's Hill, 154
St Andrew Undershaft, 142
St Anne's, Limehouse, 24
St Barnabas, Chelsea, 78
St Barnabas, King's Square, 132
St Bartholomew's Hospital, 152
  medical school, 138
St Botolph's, Bishopsgate, 144
St Bride's, Fleet Street, 154
St Columba's, Walton Street, 86
St Dunstan-in-the-East, 142
St Dunstan's, Stepney, 22
St Edmund-the-King, Lombard St, 144
St George-in-the-East, 18
St George's Field, Stepney, 22
St George's Road and Circus, 42
St George's Square, 74
St Giles Circus, 164
St James's, 78, 60
St James's Church, Bayswater, 96
St James's Church, Piccadilly, 60
St James's Palace, 6, 48, 62, 66
St James's Park, 6, 48, 50, 56, 104, 168
St James's Place, 60
St James's Square, 6, 7, 60
St James's Street, 60
St James-the-Less, 56
St John's, Smith Square, 56, 80
St John's Chapel, Park Road, 112
St John's, Waterloo, 40

St John's Wood, 112
St Katharine Cree Church, 142
St Katharine's Chapel, Regent's Park, 116
St Katharine's Dock, 18, 32, 76
St Leonard's, Shoreditch, 132
St Luke's, Old Street, 132
St Magnus the Martyr, 142
St Martin-in-the-Fields, 168
St Martin's Lane, 164
St Martin's, Ludgate Hill, 148
St Mary-at-Hill, 142
St Mary-le-Strand, 162
St Mary Magdalene, Bermondsey, 32
St Mary's, Rotherhithe, 30
St Mary Woolnoth, Lombard Street, 144
St Matthew's, Great Peter Street, 56
St Michael's, Chester Square, 64, 70
St Michael's, Cornhill, 144
St Michael's Alley, 144
St Olave, Hart Street, 142
St Pancras Church, 124
St Pancras Church, Old, 122
St Pancras Hospital, 122
St Pancras Hotel, 126
St Pancras Station, 8, 64, 122, 124, 126, 128
St Paul's, Wilton Place, 64
St Paul's Cathedral, 7, 9, 142, 148, 150, 154, 164
St Peter ad Vincula (Tower of London), 16
St Peter's, Eaton Square, 64
St Saviour's Dock, 32
St Stephen's, Vincent Square, 56
St Stephen's, Walbrook, 140
St Stephen's Chapel, Westminster, 52
Samaritan Hospital for Women, 106
Savile Row, 60
Savoy Hotel, 164
Savoy Palace, 6, 46
Savoy Theatre, 164
Science Museum, 86, 88
Scott, Sir George Gilbert, 50, 54, 56, 86, 102, 126, 144
Scott, Sir Giles Gilbert, 80, 162
Scott, J.R., 40
Scott, Sir Walter, 54
Scottish Office, 50
Sedding, J.D., 70
Selfridges, 104
Sergeant's Inn, 158
Serpentine, 90, 96
Serpentine Bridge, 90

Seven Dials, 164
Shad Thames Street, 32
Shadwell, 22
Shaftesbury, Lord, 94
Shaftesbury Avenue, 164, 166
Shakespeare, William, 34, 36, 38, 160
Shell Centre, 40, 46
Shepherd, Edward, 92
Shepherd Market, 92
Shepherd's Bush, 156
'Sherlock Holmes's London', 106
Shoe Lane, 154
Shoreditch, 36, 132, 134
Siddons, Mrs, 96
Sidney Street Siege (1911), 20
Silver Vaults, Chancery Lane, 156
Simpson, J.W., 100
Sloane Rangers, 68
Sloane Square, 70, 82
Sloane Street, 7, 68, 70, 86
slums, slum-clearance, 6, 18, 22, 30, 32, 56
Smirke, Sir Robert, 14, 130, 168
Smithfield, 142, 152
Smith Square, 56, 80
Smollett, Tobias, 34
Snowdon, Lord, 118
Soane, Sir Hans, 130
Soane, Sir John, 124, 140, 156
Soho, 156, 166
Soho Square, 166
Somerset House, 46, 162
Somers Town, 122
Southampton Row, 156
South Audley Street, 104
South Bank cultural complex, 40, 46
South Kensington, 96
South Molton Lane, 92
Southwark, 6, 34, 36, 38, 42
Southwark Bridge, 36
Southwark Cathedral, 34
Southwark Park, 30
Speakers' Corner, 90
Spencer, Herbert, 112
Spencer House, St James's, 8, 60
Spitalfields Market, 18, 134
Stanhope House, 92
Stanley Crescent, 98
Staple Inn, 156, 158
Stationers' Hall, 148
Stepney, 8, 18, 22
Stock Exchange, 144
Strachey, Lytton, 128
Strand, 6, 46, 158, 162, 164

Strand Theatre, 164
Street, G.E., 56, 96, 126, 158
Surrey Commercial Docks, 24, 30
Sussex Gardens, 96
Sussex Place, 116
Sutherland, first Duke of, 60
Sutton, Thomas, 138
Swan and Edgar's, Piccadilly, 94
Swan Theatre, 36

Tanner Street, 32
Tate Gallery, 72
Tavistock Square, 128
Tea House, Hyde Park, 90
Temple (Inner and Middle), 158, 160, 162
Temple Bar, 6, 7, 46, 148
Temple Church, 160
Temple Gardens, 158, 160
Thackeray, Thomas Makepeace, 138
Thames, river, 7, 9, 14, 20, 22, 24, 30, 32, 34, 38, 40, 46, 72, 78, 82, 104, 158
  Pimlico refuse barges, 76
  South Bank cultural complex, 40, 46
  Upper Pool, 22
  Woolwich Flood Barrier, 28
  see also dockland; Regent's Canal
Thames House, 72
Thames Tunnel, 30
Thames TV, 108
theatre, 36, 38, 40, 116, 164
Theobald's Road, 128
Thompson, Michael, 76
Thorney Island, 5, 52
Thrale, Henry, 36
Threadneedle Street, 144
Throgmorton Street, 144
Tijou, Jean, 84
Times Newspapers, 128, 154
Tite, Sir William, 140
Tottenham Court Road, 108, 128
Tower Bridge, 14, 32, 124
Tower Hamlets, 22
Tower of London, 12, 14, 16, 66
Town and Country Planning Act (1947), 8
Toynbee Hall, 18
Trade and Industry, Dept. of, 56
Trafalgar Square, 108, 166, 168
Travellers' Club, 60
Treasury, 50
Trinity House, 14
Trinity Square, 142
Turner, J.M.W., 82

Tyburn Gallows, 66, 96
Tyburn, river, 92, 106
'Tyburnia', 96, 106
Tyler, Wat, 152

Unilever House, 38
United Services Club, 60
University College, 108
Upper Grosvenor Street, 92
US Embassy, 104

Vale of Health, 120
Vanbrugh, Sir John, 26
Vaudeville Theatre, 164
Vauxhall Bridge, 72, 74
Vauxhall Bridge Road, 56
Vauxhall pleasure gardens, 72
Vickers' Building, 72
Victoria, Queen, 44, 66, 136
Victoria and Albert Museum, 86
Victoria Embankment, 38, 158
Victoria Hospital for Children, 82
Victoria Park, 22, 132
Victoria Station, 8, 10, 78
Victoria Street, 56
Vincent Street council flats, 72
Vulliamy, Lewis, 86

Walbrook, 140

Walbrook, river, 12, 140
Wallace, William, 152
Walton Street, 86
Walworth, 30, 32
Wandsworth, 82
Wandsworth Bridge, 96
Wapping, 20, 22, 30
Wardour Street, 166
Warren Street tube station, 108
Warwick Lane, 148
Waterhouse, Alfred, 88, 156, 166
Waterloo Bridge, 46, 162
Waterloo Place, 60
Waterloo Station, 34, 40, 42
Webb, Sir Aston, 66
Well Walk, 120
Wellcome Museum, 124
Wellington Road, 112
Wembley, 100
    Empire Pool, 100
    Empire Stadium, 100
Wesley's Chapel, City Road, 132
Westbourne Grove, 96
Westcheap, 140
West End, 6, 8, 10, 48, 60, 106, 124, 164
Western Pumping Station, 78
West Ham, 24
Westminster (Westminster Palace), 5, 6,
    10, 46, 48, 52, 56, 66, 72, 78, 104,
    162

administrative area, 56
    clock tower and Big Ben, 52
    Houses of Parliament, 52
    Victoria Tower, 52
Westminster Abbey, 5, 9, 52, 54, 56, 64
Westminster Bridge, 38, 46
Westminster Cathedral, 9, 56, 58
Westminster Council House and
    Library, 106
Westminster Hall, 5, 28, 52
Westminster Refuse Transfer Station, 76
Westminster School playing fields, 56
Westway, 106, 124
Whitechapel, 136
Whitechapel Art Gallery, 22
Whitechapel Bell Foundry, 136
Whitechapel Road, 136
Whitefriars' Street, 154
Whitehall (Whitehall Palace), 6, 9, 44, 46,
    48, 50, 66, 108, 166
Whitehall Court, 166
Whitehall Place, 166
White Hart Inn, Southwark, 34
White Horse Street, 92
White Tower (Tower of London), 5, 7,
    16
White's Club, 60
Wilde, Oscar, 18
Wilkins, William, 168
William I the Conqueror, King, 5, 7, 16

William II Rufus, 5, 52
William III, King, 84, 90
William IV, King, 66
Wilton Crescent, 64, 68
Wilton Place, 64, 68
Wimbledon, 44
    All England Lawn Tennis Club, 44
    Common, 44
Winfield House, Park Road, 112
Wise, Henry, 84
Woburn Place, 124
Wolsey, Thomas, Cardinal, 6, 46, 84
Woolf, Virginia and Leonard, 128, 130
Woolwich Flood Barrier, 28
Woolworth Building, Marylebone, 106
Wren, Sir Christopher, 7, 26, 54, 60, 82,
    84, 140, 142, 144, 148, 150, 154, 158
Wyatt, Benjamin, 60
Wyatt, James, 60, 64
Wyatt, Samuel, 14
Wyndham's Theatre, 164

Yevele, Henry, 54
York House, 6, 46, 62
York Place, 46, 48
York Way, 126

Zola, Emile, 78
Zoological Society Gardens, 116, 118